HEALTH IS FOR GOD

Christopher Hamel Cooke

Health is for God

by

CHRISTOPHER HAMEL COOKE

Published by Arthur James
One Cranbourne Road,
London, N10 2BT

First published in 1986
© Christopher Hamel Cooke, 1986

Published in 1986 by Arthur James Ltd.,
One Cranbourne Road, London N10 2BT, England

ISBN 85305 270 0

Printed in Great Britain by
Richard Clay (The Chaucer Press) Ltd.,
Bungay, Suffolk

FOREWORD

by Denis Duncan

Director of The Churches' Council for Health and Healing

There has been, in the Eighties, in almost every branch of the church, a recovery of the Healing Ministry as a normal part of the life, worship and witness of the Christian community. Many have embraced this significant spiritual development with enthusiasm and gladness. Others have been resistant to it and suspicious of it, uncomfortable with dramatic, emotional public healing services and afraid that expectations raised may be disappointed. It is therefore important that, within the literature of the Church's ministry of healing, there should be balance and responsibility along with a conviction that this ministry must be encompassed in prayer, founded on the Word and theologically grounded in the great doctrinal statements of the creeds.

Christopher Hamel Cooke, the Rector of St Marylebone Parish Church in London and founder of the St Marylebone Healing and Counselling Centre, has done a great deal through preaching, lecturing and personal witness to provide a proper concept of wholeness to counteract an over-emphasis on physical cure, however important that is (and it was to Jesus). He has therefore, in a notable ministry, set healing in a liturgical context (his regular service in St Marylebone combines worship, proclamation, prayer and music for the purposes of healing ministry), but he has also, as someone trained in theology and psychology, exercised an individual ministry to many in both counselling and spiritual direction. Set in a parish embracing medicine (as the Parish Church of Harley Street) and music (as the Parish Church of the Royal Academy of Music), Christopher Hamel Cooke has been able to offer a vision in which many of God's gifts of creation (a favourite theme of his, and one central to this book) can be used *together* to help people in need to be more whole. The St Marylebone Healing and Counselling Centre is a living symbol of various disciplines working in unity in the ministry of healing.

Health is for God is an important contribution to the literature on healing ministry in that it sets it in the context of Creation (a theme important to the understanding of miracle) and offers a sacramental view of healing that is of great value to 'the body of Christ', the healing community of the Risen Lord.

It is a pleasure and privilege to commend this contribution to the ministry of healing, and to express gratitude to its distinguished author for the 'vision of St Marylebone'.

June 1986

PREFACE

Health is for God. We are to seek health for His sake, and healing as a means to that end. Health ultimately means holiness, the perfection of our relationship with Him. On our journey to that goal we encounter sickness and pain. We offer it to God in the spirit of the Gethsemane prayer; we ask for what we want, but pray that His will may be done.

It is the thesis of this book that God's creative love is a present reality, the ground of our existence. It is not so much that He has made us but that He is making us. We are therefore to discern His hand and His purpose in every event of life. We are also to recognise that our prayers are part of that purpose and, ineeed, help to bring it about. So He has determined.

From our point of view things take place in a chronological order—but not from God's. For Him, who created time, all things are eternally present. So we have no need to think of divine intervention but rather of what God, from our angle, is doing next. He does not intervene; He creates this situation now. Miracles are those things which take us by surprise and cause us to wonder. This realisation has important bearing on the way we look at healing and especially the part that faith, prayer and miracle play in that process.

The Church has neglected its command to heal the sick, and its role has been usurped by others, on or even over the fringe of its life. But it is rapidly reclaiming its lost position. It must do so in an orthodox way. The word 'orthodox' comes from two Greek words which may be translated 'right opinion' or even 'straight glory'. We seek healing for our own benefit, in the service of others, but above all for God's glory.

CONTENTS

Part I

CHAPTER I

CREATION

The majority of Christian people like most of the many different denominations or 'Churches', observe the Christian Year. Some attach greater importance to it than others and so will observe the 'minor' festivals as well as the 'major' ones. Of the major ones almost all will celebrate and observe the two greatest of all, Christmas and Easter, the Birth and Resurrection of our Lord.

The date of Christ's birth is not known. December 25 is His 'official' birthday. It was a stroke of genius to choose mid-winter. The pagan world had long celebrated the 'winter solstice', the shortest day, 'Yuletide' as it came to be known. It was celebrated because, after it, the days would grow longer and the weather warmer. It was a celebration of light emerging from darkness. A pagan festival, but it was one that could be and was 'baptised' into the Christian Church. Was not the birth of Christ the ultimate celebration of light out of darkness? He whom Simeon proclaimed as a Light to lighten the Gentiles and the Glory of Israel proclaimed Himself the Light of the World.

The Queen of all the Festivals is Easter. It is more important than Christmas in the sense that the completion of any task may be deemed more important than its beginning. It is the Christian Passover or Pascal Festival, the supreme confirmation of Christ's saving work which reaches its climax on the Cross on Good Friday. The Christian Easter is still governed by the moon, not the sun; it is a moveable, not a fixed feast. It is tied to the Jewish Passover which celebrated the Exodus. The Exodus took place at the Spring full moon and the date of Easter is calculated by the same principle.

So the twin foci of the Christian Year and of our annual rehearsal of the saving events of the Incarnate life are Christmas and Easter. But there is a serious omission. The Church's year has no festival of Creation and no doubt in consequence, the doctrine of creation has been largely ignored. True, it has become one of the 'themes' in the pre-Christmas season in the revised Lectionary of both the Roman and Anglican Churches (in the Anglican Book of Common Prayer of 1662, it was the theme of the immediately pre-Lent season) and this is great gain. I suspect too that the popularity of the modern Harvest Festival (which began in 1847 at Morwenston in Cornwall, the brain-child of the Reverend R. S. Hawker the then Vicar) has something to do with the scant regard which is otherwise given to creation. Harvest Festival is indeed a celebration of creation and celebrates the 'here and now' of it. It is a Benedicite by the Church on behalf of all that God has made and is making. On behalf of nature, man praises God.

Our understanding of salvation pre-supposes an understanding of creation. It follows that our understanding of healing does so too, for healing and salvation are ultimately inseparable, and indeed, in many languages they are expressed by the same word. The New Testament concepts of salvation are based upon the Old Testament concepts of creation. The mythical accounts of creation contained in the first two chapters of the Bible enshrine many and great truths. Do they suffice as models for Christian understanding? If they do, they need to be made available in a way they have not been since it was recognised that they are not history and so are not to be treated as literally true. The rationale of Christian healing requires that we should have adequate 'models' of creation, for in healing it is what God has 'made' that is being 'mended'. It is probably true that our understanding of Christian healing does more than anything else to bring creation and salvation into synthesis, to relate them to each other in such a way that each is more clearly understood.

Now let us take from the Genesis stories what they really mean to convey. First they bear witness to the truth that God was in the beginning. Time is His creation and so He is outside and beyond time. Secondly, all that is stems from Him. The creator of the Universe is the universal creator. All that is good comes from Him, and all that we perceive as bad does so too, for there is no other source of anything. Health, sickness, pleasure and pain, joy and sorrow, know no other source, for there is no other.

Thirdly, man, humankind is made in God's image and likeness. This is not of course a physical resemblance. It means that God has given to us free will, a freedom of choice, ultimately to serve Him or disobey Him, and in so doing He has limited His own freedom. God's omnipotence is limited by our power, derived of course from Him, but also by His own will. Man has in fact chosen to rebel. We cannot explain the taint of original sin, but we can hardly fail to observe it. What God made good is no longer good. Evil permeates it and from the beginning it needed to be healed and saved. The mythical story of the Fall may not account for the Fall, but it testifies to the fact of it. Some may, perhaps most people do, reject the notion that there ever was a time before the Fall. It is of little importance. It is the fact of the universality of evil, of the comprehensiveness of man's fallen condition, that matters.

But there is a truth of profound importance that the Genesis stories tend to obscure. In some editions of the Authorised Version of the Bible, at the top of the page on which Genesis begins, there is written the date of creation—4004 BC. This date was arrived at by Archbishop Ussher (1581–1656). After a very careful analysis of the biblical evidence and indeed a dating of the whole of the Old Testament, he worked back through the recorded 'history' to determine that that was the year when it all began. There are still those who refer to 1985 not only as 'the year of our Lord' but also as 'Anno Lucis 5989'—'the year of Light'.

From a fundamentalist standpoint, such people insist that the opening chapters of Genesis are history. When occasionally doubts are cast by modern science on the Darwinian theory of evolution, such people imagine that they have been right all the time. But Genesis 1 and 2 are not history, whether or not the theory of evolution is true. They are not history because those who wrote them did not write them as such, did not themselves 'believe' them in the way that credence is given to a true account of an actual occurrence. Archbishop Ussher was not so much at fault for his arithmetic. It was not that he should have been thinking in terms of many millions rather than a few thousands of years. It was that his whole concept of creation was mistaken. *Creation did not take place thousands or millions of years ago; it is taking place now.* Upon this contention much of what follows is based.

Because man lives in time and measures all that happens in his life by months and years, his mind is forever trying to conceive a beginning and an end. God is outside time and for Him everything is eternally present. The word 'time' is not, as it were, in the vocabulary of God. Everything for Him is 'here' and 'now', and we are held in being by His creative activity. We may forget Him, but if He were to forget us, we should immediately cease to be.

We shall, of course, for ever go on wondering about how everything began, and why. What did God create out of? Who made God? If we can measure time backwards, we shall always be trying to get back further still. But it will ultimately be a profitless exercise just because it cannot be ultimate. The finite mind, conditioned by time and space, simply cannot get back and behind them both to arrive at an explanation of how everything began. But if we accept that God's creation is now, that God is making us and all that is around us, we shall be able to find working answers to the questions that we really need to ask—need, because our well-being depends upon the answers. Without those answers we have no sense of purpose, no meaning to our existence, no interpretation of what is going on, in us and around us; and, perhaps, no incentive to live.

Let us refer again to the Christian Year. It begins with Advent, a period of preparation for the first of the two great festivals, the Nativity of our Lord Jesus Christ. The word 'Advent' stems from the same Latin word (*venire, to come*) as does the word 'adventure'. This is a very helpful word and a most useful concept in our understanding of the meaning of life. Advent refers to Christ's adventure, to His coming to the world. We may well regard the whole of life as a series of arrivals, of coming to find things which God has put in our way.

I can remember an elderly cousin doing this with my children. She used to invite us over when they were small and she would hide sweets in all sorts of places in the garden and then let them loose to go and find them. In a sense that is what God has done. He has filled His universe with good things and He has left us to discover them and to find them out. Health comes in the finding of the good things that God has so liberally distributed throughout His universe. The joy of discovery is one of the greatest joys God gives us. When we lose our capacity for discovery and our ability to go on discovering, we are liable to become sick. Indeed such loss is a kind of sickness. So life is adventure. God creates in us and for us the 'advents' which belong to each one of us. Life is a journey of discovery.

The notion of journey is all important to the Christian understanding of the why and wherefore of creation. We shall look, in a later chapter, at the journey's end, at man's destiny. To lose sight of the ultimate goal is to make nonsense of the journey. But preoccupation with that goal means that we miss the meaning and the joy of the innumerable staging posts along the way and the pleasure of travelling itself. Man differs from man in a wide variety of ways. Some are black and some are white; some are rich and some are poor; some are beautiful

and some are ugly; some are young and some are old, but the
greatest difference of all is that between those who believe
that life is a journey and those who do not believe there is a
journey to be made. It is the maxim of the Christian that 'here
we have no abiding city, but we seek one hereafter' (Hebrews
13, 14).

The writer of the Epistle to the Hebrews was echoing a very
ancient belief of the Hebrew people. It is expressed early in
the book of Genesis, although not always recognised as such.
It is the story of Cain and Abel. The sacrifice by Abel of one
of his flock was acceptable to God. Cain's sacrifice of the
produce of the land was not. A later writer tried to give the
story a moral connotation ('sin croucheth at the door', Genesis
4, 7). But originally it was a story extolling the nomadic life
and condemning the settled village life where man stayed put,
planted seeds and harvested their yield. The nomadic life was
held up as the ideal because it was a constant reminder that
'here we have no abiding city'. The story in Genesis, reinforced
in Hebrews, is likewise a constant reminder of the 'disease'
that stems from preoccupation with worldly possessions, from
man's obsession to be getting and holding on to temporal
goods. He loses his sense of journey; he wants to live here
forever; he is indeed unhealthy.

The religious concept of poverty, to which members of religious communities particularly subscribe, is the spirit in
which all Christians are meant to live. It is about 'travelling
light', about a healthy detachment from possessions, about
simplicity in our attitude to them. We, in fact, enjoy them all
the more if we hold them in true perspective. They are solaces
along the way, not the be-all and end-all of our existence.

It is my contention that God creates man for adventure and
sets him on a journey. He is to see himself as a pilgrim. But
he is not an isolated one. The next chapter will attempt to
look at his relationships on his journey and to show that health
has to do with being healthy in relationship, not merely with
one's own body, mind and spirit.

CHAPTER II

RELATIONSHIP

Every human creature born into this world is the fruit of a physical and emotional relationship. The human baby is conceived in relationship. I want now to explore relationships and to show how we can be well or sick in all of them.

We can conveniently divide relationships into four: *to things*; *to other people*; *to ourselves*; *to God*. My own shorthand for this is to describe them as being *downwards*, *outwards*, *inwards* and *upwards*. Each of them may be considered both from the point of view of the individual and also collectively or socially.

We are all related to things and we are usually looking downwards when we are specifically so engaged, as I am, as I write, with pen in hand. My being so engaged immediately makes the first point. Am I healthily related to my pen? Do I use it so that I may be easily read, so that it is a pleasure to the reader to see my calligraphy? The word calligraphy means beautiful writing. The pursuit of beauty, if not its attainment, is generally accepted to belong to man's true well being. To be content with 'ugly' writing, illegible or untidy writing, is not healthy. The surgeon and the motor mechanic will have still greater need to be in harmony with the implements in their hands. Their not being so may cause injury or death.

In the exercise of relationship to things, we may also include the abstract, time. We may look at our use of time, our priorities in the allocation of it, our punctuality. These all have to do with a certain kind of health or with a certain kind of disease. Until there is health in these areas of our lives we need, and should be seeking, healing.

At the corporate level, the same questions need to be asked.

Man and his environment is a relationship which has gone
sadly wrong. Humankind exploits the rest of creation, and threat-
ens with extinction certain rare species. We consume the fossil
fuels and mar the countryside in the process. We build ugly
cities and subordinate our love of beauty and our concern for
our fellow men to our greed or our urge for power. Every
individual and every society of man are sick in their relationship to things and to their environment. The need to be
healed is for ever with them. All along life's journey, all
through human history the disease, the sickness, is evident.
Christian prophecy proclaims that need and offers the
remedy.

The division of our relationships is artificial and only done
for the purposes of analysis. Discord in any one area must
upset the harmony of the whole. So our misuse of things will
affect our relationship with other people, our relationship
outwards. Man is born into community, into a family which is
part of a larger society, village, suburb or town, which is part
of the nation, which is part of the whole family of man. Each
individual has many relationships and so does each society.
Many of those who become sick in this area of their lives do
so because they have no significant relationship with any other
human being. The psychiatrist to whom they may turn for
help cannot cure them in isolation; they may relate to him as a
therapist, but his work is not done unless the client can there-
after begin to make satisfactory relationships in his own
environment.

His environment may of course itself be inimical. He might
learn to relate to it at the cost to his health in another area.
Our Lord Himself could not relate to the scribes and the
pharisees. If He had, He might not have been crucified. What
was needed was not a change in Him, but a change in the
society to which He belonged. So it may be for anyone.

Many of those who need counselling are ill because they are
well! By refusing to conform to the norms of their peers,
because they regard those norms as evil or sinful, they find it

difficult to relate to those around them. They become isolated and lonely and, in consequence, depressed and anxious. It is no answer to persuade them to abandon their deeply held principles. To do so would make for an immediately more healthy relationship with those around them, but at the cost of their inner peace, their self-esteem, their moral integrity. So indeed it was for Christ. So will it be, very often, for his disciples.

The healing of relationships with other people is not merely a pastoral concern. It is also a prophetic one. It is about changing other people. It is about altering an environment. 'Honour among thieves' may inhibit the informer. But the thief who repents of his thieving may lose his friends in his withdrawal from their pursuits. He may suffer loneliness and loss in the process. He sacrifices a lesser health to a greater one. Integrity and honesty are not to be sacrificed to secure companionship or to overcome loneliness.

The Church has a part to play not only in comforting the lonely and in challenging the evil in society. It also serves to provide an alternative environment where healthy relationships can be made. In this sense it may stand over against the community in which it is set.

The Church is itself an extended family, in which healthy relationships can be made. The Church is never, of course, perfect. It is itself a diseased society, but it will be different because it has an awareness of its imperfection and penitence for it. It will therefore be a welcoming and reconciling community, capable of bringing this kind of healing to those who seek its membership—perhaps in the first place for this reason alone. The Church is also concerned, and very significantly so, for those who do not belong. It was Archbishop William Temple who described the Church as the only organisation which exists for the benefit of those who are not its members. Its reconciling work in the area of human relationships is vital to its own healthy existence.

The Samaritans may be cited as evidence of this—founded

by a parish priest, to serve at first the desperate in his own environment, it has become one of the great pieces of social outreach of the century. Man has to live in love and harmony with his neighbour. The love may not be total, the harmony may not be complete. The tolerance of a certain measure of disease has to be accepted though never embraced, but the quest for perfection must never be abandoned nor hope in its achievement be lost.

Relationships outward also must have a corporate as well as a personal dimension. A row over the garden fence is not different in principle from civil war or world war. Both stem from man's inability to relate to his fellows. He desires peace but not the means of achieving it. He wants harmony on his own terms. He is blinded by an astonishing degree of assurance of the justice of his own position and the error and wickedness of that of his opponent. Corporate penitence seems even more elusive than individual repentance. For a country to say 'we were wrong' is rare in the extreme. The individual often seems powerless when confronted by war or civil strife. He longs to see and do something about what he sees as evidently wicked and self-destructive. But in truth he has no right to criticise if he is at cross purposes with the person next door or has fallen out with a member of his own family because he disapproves of his way of life.

Yet peace is not peace if it is bought at any price. Evil is properly to be confronted if justice is to be done. It is only in justice that true peace can subsist. The just war and the just revolution remain valid to the Christian conscience. Evil there will always be, but greater evils may stem from their abandonment. If individuals cannot be healthily related to unhealthy neighbours, nor can peoples or nations. There is a corporate integrity as well as a personal one and it cannot be sacrificed at the altar of appeasement.

The third relationship is of man to himself. Again this cannot be seen in isolation from the other relationships except for the purposes of analysis. We relate to ourselves—to our bodies, to our minds, to our feelings. A baby born with a physical deformity has to learn to relate to a misshapen body and to the implications of it in terms of other relationships. The reverse may be the problem. The boy or girl with obvious physical advantages may have to combat pride or vanity and to develop an attitude of mind which is just as necessary to his/her well-being as in the case of the handicapped child.

One of the preoccupations of men and women in the twentieth century in western civilisation is with the shape of their bodies, through over-indulgence in food and drink. The body, which is meant to be subservient to the mind, is allowed to rule the appetite, and the harmony between mind and body is impaired. Man has to learn to cope with the physical ailments that beset his body, with growing old and ultimately seeing his body perish. He has to live too with his thoughts and with his feelings, with his mind and with his heart. He wants to be at peace with himself but peace often eludes him. He becomes depressed or anxious. A psychiatrist will generally not have the time to give him the treatment which might lead to his self-reconciliation. He may prescribe tablets to alleviate symptoms but no more. Nor can he do more unless he has the conviction for himself to help his client find a sense of purpose, a destiny to which his life might lead.

Not everyone who lacks that sense of purpose experiences disease within himself but for many it is the real cause of their sickness. The psychiatrist can find nothing wrong, for the diagnosis is beyond his competence. So we must learn to live at peace not only with the mechanical parts of our bodies, but with the thinking and feeling parts as well. Of course the word 'parts' is inappropriate. It is used solely for the purpose of analysis. Holism knows no distinction of parts. A person is his body, is his mind, is his spirit. Perspective may be preferred to 'parts'—but language cannot do justice to wholeness, to the integrity of the person and at the same time analyse that person.

Does this relationship also have a corporate dimension?

Indeed it does. Societies have a life of their own which is different from the sum of their parts. A class of children in school will often have a corporate character which seems not to stem from any individual member of it. The same is true of a cricket club, a political party or even a whole nation. It begins with the family itself where the corporate expression of its life seems to have a dynamic of its own which needs to be understood by all who are its members. It is often far from being harmonious, from being healthy. It needs healing at a corporate level which is different from the treatment of any individual member of it.

The fourth relationship, upwards, of man to God, is to the Christian not only the most important, the one that is top of the categories, but it overarches or undergirds and interprets all of the others. So the Christian regards relationship with God as an essential part of being truly human. It is not an added and voluntary extra. That many people think so is evidenced by the frequency of such statements as 'I'm not a religious kind of person'. But there are no religious kinds of people. To the Christian, man is made in the image and likeness of God. It is not as it were that some people have souls and some an empty space where the soul ought to be. We believe with St Augustine that man is made for God and that his soul is restless until it rests in Him. Moreover, we believe that since all of us, and not some of us, are made in God's image, that we are all likenesses of God, that we see God's likeness in each other, and reflect something of God Himself in our contacts and our daily encounters. To believe this is to desire to ensure that the reflection that we give is one which will reflect God as perfectly as possible and mar His image as little as possible. Only our Lord perfectly reflected God. In Him alone the image was not impaired. He was the perfect reflection of God's true being (Hebrews 1, 3). In the hall of mirrors at a fun fair we see a grossly distorted picture of ourselves. In real life we all reflect an image of God, but distorted.

Healing is about curing that distortion. Salvation is about attaining that image in its perfection.

The concept of sin is not a popular one and it has been greatly misused and misunderstood, but, by definition, anything that separates man from God and distorts His image is sin and causes him to be diseased in this the ultimate of his relationships. Total or perfect harmony with God is perfect sanctity or holiness. Health, holiness and wholeness are closely related words which remind us that healing and salvation are ultimately the same. For healing that does not include the achievement of perfect harmony with God is not complete. He is not whole who is not holy.

The corporate dimension of the fourth relationship is most evident to the Christian. The Bible, Old and New Testaments alike, knows nothing of private religion but always sets it in a corporate or congregational context. The catechism of the Church of England Book of Common Prayer says of Baptism 'therein I was made a member of Christ and the child of God'. The indefinite article in the first clause is contrasted with the definite in the second. I am *a* member and *the* child. God knows me and loves me, by name, as if I were His only child. But He sees me as one of His family, a member of His body, one of countless thousands, in paradise and on earth, belonging to Him and belonging to my fellow citizens. We are siblings, all, of the self-same father.

It is worth remembering that when our Lord commanded His disciples to become fishers of men, He was speaking to those accustomed to nets and not to lines. They were not to land one fish at a time but enclose a shoal of them all together. That the Church should preach personal salvation goes without saying, but it must always do so in the context of its corporate existence.

In Victorian England the emphasis on individual salvation suggested that man could be in right relationship with God on his own and it is fascinating that the fathers of modern psychology also practised their therapy in a one-to-one relationship which is now seen to be partial and one-sided unless it is accompanied by some kind of group therapy.

Furthermore the Christian must never give countenance to the idea that his witness must only be to individuals as such or to the individual in the context of the Church. Every secular society from the smallest to the greatest exists in God's world for God's glory. When the Church is bidden to keep out of politics for instance, blasphemy is uttered. There is no area of human activity that is not meant to be subject to the will of God and to His laws. It is the business of the Christian as an individual and the Church as a corporate body to proclaim that truth and act upon it. God is not the Lord of Sunday only but of every day. His house is not the church building only, but is every home. His people are not the congregation merely, but all mankind. His supper is not just the Eucharist, but every meal.

Let us now take up consideration of the Sacraments.

CHAPTER III

THE SACRAMENTS

The Catechism in the Church of England Book of Common Prayer defines 'Sacrament' as 'an outward and visible sign of an inward and spiritual grace'. The definition may only serve to make a difficult concept seem more difficult still. But in fact the concept is not only easy to understand but is taken for granted by all of us in everyday life. We may not call them sacraments but we all use 'sign language' to give abstract things a substantial reality. Take for instance the hand shake; it is an outward sign of the inward grace we call friendship. Friendship is an abstract noun; you cannot draw a picture of it. But when two people shake hands, they not only exchange a sign of friendship but they have an actual experience of friendship. The sign is an effectual sign; it not only demonstrates, it also creates and enhances—and we all understand it without need for explanation. To stand when the National Anthem is played, to bow one's head when a funeral passes by are comparable signs of loyalty and respect. Many others can be instanced.

The human being expresses himself thus because that is what human nature itself is like. The body expresses what is going on in the heart and mind because these three 'parts' are inextricably linked. They are what we are. Sometimes the body expresses what is going on inside involuntarily, and sometimes, as we have seen, voluntarily. The blush of embarrassment, the trembling in fear—these are involuntary expressions over which we have no control. They express physically our thoughts and our emotions.

Every human being is an outward and visible sign of God Himself—an *icon* or *image* of God—because that is what we

are and why we are. God made man in His own image. The
Christian faith, following the faith of Judaism, begins there.
It goes on to say that although every man is an image of God,
only one such image perfectly expressed the Godhead, in so
far as the Godhead can be so expressed. The Incarnation is
the perfect and the ultimate expression of God's own person,
'the word made flesh'. We are all sons and daughters of God.
But to the question, What kind of a Son of God is Jesus of
Nazareth?, the answer comes, 'the one perfect and unique Son,
the express image of God's glory'.

The sacramental principle is not therefore either difficult
or abstruse. It is simple and self-evident. We express ourselves
to God, and He to us, through effectual signs, the bodily
gesture or action speaking to us of the hidden things of the
mind or spirit.

In what follows I shall be using the word 'symbol' as a
collective noun for sacraments and I would like first to enlarge
upon its meaning. It comes from two Greek words σύν and
βολή which mean 'throw together'. A symbol is therefore an
agent of harmony, of reconciliation, of reintegration. Its opposite is the work of the devil, the diabolic, which comes from
the Greek words διά and βολή, meaning to throw apart. So we
see that the sacraments are indeed the agencies of God,
designed to combat the forces of evil, bringing peace and
harmony wherever there is hostility or discord.

Our Christian discipleship depends upon Faith and upon its
outward and visible sign, Baptism. The symbolic washing
(*Baptizo*—I wash) is a symbol of cleansing, of regeneration. It
is usually accompanied by other symbolic acts—the anointing
with holy oil (christening), the 'burial' in the water and the
rising from it which emerging from total immersion represent.
The font is the 'tomb' into which we are buried with Christ
and from which tomb we rise with Him. It is also the womb
of the Church from which we are born into active and live
membership. We are given a candle to remind us that Christ is
the light of the world and that we who have thus passed from

darkness to light are meant to shine in the world with His reflected light. The initiation ceremony abounds with symbols, all of which are meant to impress upon us the meaning of Faith and the implications of it.

Baptism is a healing sacrament. It speaks of man's need of grace. If administered to a baby, it is a proclamation of original sin and of Christ's universal salvation. Why do some people find the concept of original sin so difficult? No doctrine of the Church is more self-evident. A small boy in his class at school was asked by the teacher what was the first thing he must do if he was to receive God's forgiveness. He replied, 'Go out and do some sins.' But he was wrong. We sin because we are sinners; we are not made sinners by the act of sinning. Everyone born into the world has the disposition, the kind of nature, that will inevitably lead into sin and so to alienation from God. At Baptism, we proclaim what God in Christ has done to make a remedy available—and we lay claim upon it. So our Healing begins at Baptism.

The sacrament of the Church which is specifically concerned with Healing is that of Unction, and related to it, the lesser sacramental act, the laying-on-of-hands. In the Church of England the teaching is that there are seven Sacraments, Baptism, Holy Communion, Confirmation, Penance, Holy Matrimony, Holy Unction and Holy Orders. Two of these—the first two—are regarded as 'generally', that is universally, necessary. The remaining five are appropriate to some, are 'particular' rather than 'universal'. In addition to the seven there are many lesser sacramental acts derived from or related to the others, such as the ring in marriage, the anointing in baptism, the stole in ordination. The outward sign in Holy Unction is oil which was originally itself medicinal and later became the symbol of healing. The Good Samaritan poured oil and wine into the wounds of the man who fell among thieves. The general practice of the Church, though by no means the universal practice (and there is no reason why the symbolism should be rigidly applied) is that Holy Unction is administered to a sick person once only for a specific physical, mental or spiritual sickness. It is a deliberate submission of that sickness to the love, mercy and judgment of God. It is a prayer for healing; it is a prayer that God's will may be known and done. The priest who administers the sacrament—or the layman in certain circumstances—will usually have prepared the patient for his reception of the sacrament, will have counselled him and prayed with him. After the event he will likewise be available to the patient to follow the event with further counselling. The sacrament may be administered privately or in the context of the Eucharist or in a Healing Service.

The laying-on-of-hands may subsequently be given as a 'renewal' of the grace of unction, just as it is given to many people who may seek only this 'lesser' sacramental act. For the laying-on-of-hands is very widely used; it is used ever increasingly in specific Healing Services where perhaps all the members of the congregation may come forward to receive this blessing. We know that none of us is wholly well for each has need of healing in some area of his or her life. Some will come forward to receive the laying-on-of-hands for another person. We can offer ourselves for the ministry vicariously. Members of a particular African tribe, when they take their brother to the doctor, say 'I am sick in my brother'. The ministrant at the laying-on-of-hands may not know the need of the person who kneels before him and will probably not have counselled him beforehand.

It is important to make it known at a Healing Service that counselling is available to anyone who wants it. Sometimes great harm can be done if people go away, having received this ministry, not perhaps having had their expectations healed first. Subsequent help may be of vital importance in such, and many other, contexts.

The laying-on-of-hands is quite commonly given when prayers are said at the conclusion of a Christian Counselling session. Many of the clergy normally lay hands when they pray with a patient in hospital or when they give the blessing after administering Holy Communion. The experience of touch is the experience of an enacted prayer and speaks of the love and compassion of God mediated through His minister.

The Sacrament of Penance is also a Sacrament of Healing. In the formality of the Confessional, or in the informality of a pastoral conversation, the priest, the minister or the Christian counsellor brings the assurance of God's pardon and healing to the penitent. It is part of the very essence of ministerial priesthood to do this. We are not here concerned to examine the varied approaches of different denominations. They all agree that the Gospel of our Lord Jesus Christ is a Gospel of healing and salvation. It is proclaimed not only from a pulpit, but to all who seek it for the quietening of their own conscience, for their spiritual progress on their pilgraimage through life, for their healing, whenever they are hurt and damaged.

The confession of sin is the confession of symptoms. They can be and are forgiven. But it is to the underlying sinfulness that attention needs to be addressed, of which particular offences are the immediate evidence. Sin and sickness are not directly related in the sense that sickness is often thought of as punishment for sin. This is a common error which needs by many to be unlearned. The God in Whom we believe is not a vindictive, a punishing God. But nevertheless it is because of sin, the fact of original sin, tainting all humanity, and because of sins, our own and other people's, that we often become sick. Healing is as much part of the process of this sacrament as is forgiveness. This is simply because healing and salvation are ultimately inseparable, indeed are the same thing.

The grace of Baptism is renewed in the Eucharist. Though Holy Unction may be the deliberate submission of a particular sickness to the mercy of God, the Eucharist is the general submission of all that we are to God. We submit our joys as well as our sorrows, our thankfulness as well as our grievances. We do so that God may bless all that accords with His Holy will, forgive all that is at variance with it, and supply all that is wanting. Let us now see how it works.

First we must observe that the pattern of the Eucharistic Liturgy is usually divided into two parts, generally called the Liturgy of the Word and the Liturgy of the Sacrament. In the former part the Bible is read, usually from the Old Testament, from one of the Epistles and from the Gospel. The word is expounded from the pulpit. The proclamation of the Word is also a healing medium. It brings consolation, it mediates joy, it speaks of the love of God. It also brings challenge and perhaps rebuke—both of which are conducive to man's true healing.

The ministry of the Sacrament begins at the Offertory and is an enactment—something done rather than something said. We 'do this', as Christ commanded. We do what He did in the Upper Room on the night before He died. We do it to re-member Him. He did four things—and so do we. He took, He blessed, He broke and He gave. But to understand what He did we must also look back, back into the Jewish sacrificial principle. For this was done in the context of the Passover, done when our Lord and His disciples with countless other pilgrims had returned to Jerusalem to offer the Passover sacri-fice. It could only be offered in the Temple at Jerusalem and nowhere else in the world. This was Jewish Law. To the Temple, all Jews who possibly could made their way for the Passover.

The Passover was the occasion that marked the release of the Jewish people from slavery in Egypt. Moses had led the people out of the wilderness and ultimately to the Promised Land. He had done so after God had beset the Egyptians with plagues. The last of these had been the slaying of each first-born son in every Egyptian home. The Jewish houses were 'passed over' by the avenging angel, because their doorposts were marked with the blood of the sacrificial lamb, slain by each family before the flight from Egypt. Christ was the Lamb of God; slain to bring about our spiritual exodus from sin and to bring us to the promised land of His Kingdom. We are marked with His blood that we may be saved from the fate that we deserve, and we are set free. The Christian Passover, the Eucharist, is not fully intelligible unless it is seen against the background of the Jewish festival at which it was first enacted, and against the background of Calvary, where Christ was actually slain, His body given for us and His blood shed for us.

When the Jew went to the Temple to offer sacrifice, he went with simple intent. He took his lamb and he said to the priest: 'Slay this for me'. It was not the death of the lamb that he was concerned to achieve, but rather the release of its life. To the Jew, the life is in the Blood. That is why Jews to this day will not eat meat unless it is especially killed so that there is no blood left in the carcase. To consume the blood is totally abhorrent to the Jew. (That is why some of his disciples turned their back on our Lord when he talked to them about 'drinking His blood' (John 6).) So the Jew saw the life of the Lamb return to God. He identified himself with his gift and so offered his own life to God. This 'vicarious offering' is not a difficult concept. We all accept it in everyday life. The presents that we give each other, at birthday or Christmas, are 'with love from', that is, they represent the giver. The gift and the giver are not separate. They are inextricably linked.

So when we go to the Eucharist, we offer the Christian sacrifice, we go to offer Christ to the Father on our behalf. We so do because that is what Christ did. He offers Himself for us—and we must offer ourselves with Him.

> *Look Father, look on his anointed face,*
> *And only look on us as found in him;*
> *Look not on our misusings of thy grace*
> *Our prayer so languid and our faith so dim*
> *For lo between our sins and their reward,*
> *We set the passion of thy son our Lord.*

So at the offertory, we do the first of the four things that our Lord did. We take bread. The priest takes it from us—his hands are our hands. Usually it is carried to the priest from the body of the Church—which makes the point that it is the offering of the people. It is as if each one of us were to step out of our seats, place our morsel of bread on the patten, our drop of wine in the chalice and say, 'Bless this for me.' It is not merely my gift that is on the altar. It is *me*. I offer myself vicariously, figuratively. I am there, with all my sins, with all my joys, with all my hopes, with all my fears. All that I am is there and all that I have.

The second action of the Eucharist is the blessing—the consecration. Jesus, having taken the bread, gave thanks. Over it, He said, 'This is my body' and 'This is my blood'. Just as at Bethlehem or rather at the Annunciation, God took human flesh and became incarnate, so at the Eucharist He takes bread and wine and they become the vehicles of His presence with us. What was my gift, representing me, now becomes the body and blood of the Lord. He is on the altar and Him the Father can and does accept, because His offering is perfect and complete. But His offering is also my offering, my hand is in His, He dwells in me and I in Him. I, the unacceptable, become acceptable and accepted because I am reconciled to God in and through Him.

The third action is the breaking of the bread. Practically it must be broken because it is to be shared. But the fraction, as it is called, also reminds us of the cost to our Lord Jesus Christ. Our salvation was not achieved in the Upper Room but on Golgotha. God could create man just by saying 'Let there be'. But his redemption cost God, the Son of God, His Passion and His death—and the bread is broken to remind us that it was so. It reminds us too that there is, and will be, a cross in the heart of God so long as there is one soul for whom He must suffer.

Finally we go to the altar. We go to receive our Lord in Holy Communion—communion with Him and with one another. We receive back the gifts we originally made, restored and renewed. The transformation is not merely of bread and wine into the body and blood of Christ. It is the transformation of each one of us; the marred and scarred image of God which each of us is, is restored and renewed and revived. We become true likenesses of God, more and more, and we are sent out of the church to become that which we now are, to realise our potential, to be 'other christs'.

The Eucharist is indeed, with Baptism, the supreme sacrament of healing. It takes all of us and opens us up to God, that He may bless what is good, forgive what is not, and supply all that is wanting. Unlike Baptism, the once and for all proclamation of our need for forgiveness and salvation and of God's power to grant and supply our need, the Eucharist is often repeated. It is our daily bread. It is our constant renewal. It is our growing and our maturing into the fullness of our discipleship.

CHAPTER IV

THE VALUE OF
PETITION AND INTERCESSION

An evaluation or explanation of intercessory prayer demands the acceptance of certain presuppositions. It requires firstly a belief in the existence of God; secondly, a belief that a relationship between Him and His human creatures is not only possible but also an actuality; thirdly, it is necessary to believe that the process of praying can and does actually make a difference. It is the third of these contentions that we now explore.

The natural scientist who says he has no belief in God and sees no reason why he should have is unlikely to be convinced by anything that claims to be a rationale of the value of petition and intercession. The fact is that God's existence cannot be demonstrated by the processes customarily used in the natural sciences, any more than it can be disproved by those processes. It can however, be fairly stated that there is a vast amount of evidence for believing in God and that men and women down the ages of history in their multitude have lived and died for such a belief. Christianity is all about a particular view of the nature of God and of the way He has and does relate to His creation.

Christianity tells us that the God Who made us is the Father of our Lord Jesus Christ. His nature is best perceived in our understanding of the person and work of Jesus Christ. The Christian therefore cannot believe anything about God which is incompatible with that revelation. If the Christian believes that God acts, he must believe that He acts characteristically, acts as Jesus Christ acted. It was Jesus Christ Who taught His disciples to pray 'Our Father'. He taught us therefore to think of God as a loving Father. We may think that Jesus ran no small risk in teaching us so—for not all who hear that teaching have any knowledge of a loving human father, or mother. All such people are at some disadvantage in not having experienced the model which Jesus poses. They have to derive their understanding from some kind of substitute. The challenge to human parenthood implicit in our Lord's use of this model must be evident. It behoves every Christian father to look at what kind of a model he presents to his children for their understanding of God Himself. What the best of human fathers would do or not do, God would do or not do. The level of His operation may be vastly different and infinitely more complex—but the principle admits of no exception.

The little child may be baffled or even hurt by the response that the human father makes to him. I remember numerous occasions when my children were small how they would clamour to be allowed to have something or do something. Banging with their little fists on my knees they would plead their cause angrily and vociferously. I often had to say 'No' and ignore their sorrow and displeasure. Every father and mother has experienced the same thing. And every father and mother knows that the child will eventually learn that his father acted characteristically, acted lovingly, however seemingly it was not so. God may deny us many things. We may be disappointed and even angry. But we must never lose hold of our conviction that God is our loving heavenly Father—and acts always 'in character'. What He denies us is as loving as what He grants us, and must be accepted as such.

God is; God is our Father. We believe that we have or can have a relationship with Him comparable to that of a child to his parent. Do we also believe that our asking that things may happen can make any difference to their doing so?

Before we look further at this question, let us put petitionary and intercessory prayer—for that is what this question is all about—into its prayerful context.

Prayer is *not* first and foremost a *useful* activity. The first

question to ask about prayer is *not*, does it work? Indeed, it is
better to start with the very bold assertion that prayer is a
useless activity! By that bold assertion, we assert that prayer is
an end in itself and not primarily a means to another end.
Prayer is an activity of love—and love is not something we do
because it is useful! Consider it at the human level. A man
may love a woman and propose marriage to her. He will not
plead the advantages that will be his or hers because of his
love. There may be many and he may not be unmindful of
them. But he will think of them as 'by-products' and not as
the reason for loving. Love is an end, not a means—and so is
prayer. We are to pray because we love God, and because we
believe that He Loves us. We are to pray perhaps because we
only want to love Him—or even because we wish we wanted
to. We stand rebuked indeed if we pray only because we
thereby seek some advantage.

But just as in a loving human relationship, there are advantages, so there are in our relationship with God. Within the
context of His love for us and our seeking to love Him too, we
may, and indeed are encouraged to ask. Of course, our praise
and worship, our contemplation of Him, of His love and of
His glory, come first. Our praise and thanksgiving take priority
over our requests. We shall have many things to say before we
ask for anything and we shall ask for others before we ask for
ourselves. But ask we shall, and we shall be right to do so.

We shall be right because a father who loves his children
likes to be asked—and we believe it is so with God. We shall
be right because our asking demonstrates our dependence upon
God and our acknowledgement of that dependence. Whatever
intermediary there may be between God and ourselves, the
fact remains that everything comes from Him. The grace at
mealtimes is a simple example. We are fed by many intermediaries—the farmer, the miller, the baker, the transporter,
etc.—but only God can give us bread.

We shall be right because prayer is the interplay between
God's will and our own. We remember that we do have free

will. It is God's special gift to every member of His human creation. No other part of it is so endowed. That is what we mean when we say that God made man in His own image. He gave us free will and in so doing, relinquished a little of His own. We are not to believe that we must take the literal meaning out of the word gift. If God gave it, He no longer has it. So when we pray we are surrendering our free will back to God Who gives it, and two things may happen. Most obviously we shall be enabling God to bring our wills into conformity with His. It can be properly said of petition and intercession that in the process we learn to want what we get rather than to get what we want! We learn to accept God's will for us. The classic example is Christ in Gethsemane where He prayed that the 'cup might pass' from Him, but He went on to pray 'Nevertheless, not my will but thine be done'. So His will is the will of His Father, in the relationship of prayer between them.

Let it be added too that we are meant to let God know what we want! It is not sufficient to pray 'Thy will be done'. We must first pray for what we want and hope will happen—as Jesus did. Why? Because otherwise our praying is unreal. We are not appearing before God as we really are; we are hiding or masking what we really do feel or are thinking. God would never wish us to do that, and if we do it we shall not be properly exposing our wants to God—so that He can either grant them, if that is His will, or correct them, if it is not. If we do not expose our wants, we may feel them denied but not corrected and healed. By making them known we enable Him, where it is appropriate for us, to teach us what we should be wanting and what we should not. The Gethsemane prayer is always our model.

But there is another side to intercession. If it is primarily to bring our minds into line with God, yet it may sometimes be the means by which we change His! This is a bold, and to some may seem an outrageous, suggestion. Yet if it is true that in giving man—every man—free will, God thereby limits His own, it must follow that, the limitation of His freedom which He voluntarily makes, limits His freedom of action too. Because we use our free wills to rebel against Him, or to ignore Him, things happen which God would not have happen. We call these happenings *sins*. If we return to God in voluntary prayer, for the furtherance of His kingdom, we are, as it were, providing Him with the raw material of His creative purposes. God did not create the world a long time ago. He is creating it now. At His disposal are the free wills of those who submit to Him. So this can now happen, which without that surrender could not happen. We enable God.

Of course it is, strictly speaking, absurd to talk of God changing His mind. Since all things are eternally present to Him, He knows our prayers before we offer them. But His foreknowledge is no more detrimental to the freedom with which they are offered than His memory of them after the event. God's foreknowledge and God's memory are our words for describing His eternal awareness of all things. For Him there is no past and no future. So prayer changes things, because that is how God acts. Intercession and petition are a vitally important fact of the prayer life of every Christian— and nowhere more importantly than in the realm of healing. To pray for the sick and to pray for ourselves in sickness is a very important activity indeed.

We must say a word to demonstrate the equal importance of petition-prayer for ourselves and intercession—prayer for other people. The latter depends for its understanding upon our capacity for realising our interdependence, our belonging to one another, our belief that 'no man is an island'; we are not only the 'Body of Christ' knit together with the saints in one communion and fellowship, we are, at the natural level, 'members of one another'. You will not intercede on behalf of other people if you do not believe and comprehend this. If you do believe it you will NOT need to be encouraged to pray for others. Your prayers for them will be as natural as your love for them—and not essentially different.

CHAPTER V

FAITH

The Churches' ministry of healing is often called 'Faith Healing'. Because our Lord so often used the word 'faith' in connection with his works of healing, this is understandable. It can also be very misleading.

A patient in an orthopaedic ward, a man of considerable intelligence as well as religious commitment said to me, 'If I had enough faith I would not need to be in this hospital.' Yet we are told that faith the 'size' of a mustard seed is sufficient to move a mountain. It does—but only if God wants the mountain moved. Because pain and sickness, the mountains of sorrow and disability in a person's life are not always moved, either God's power or the patient's faith is called into question. Is that how we should believe? I am sure that it is not.

'I wish I had your faith.' Every priest and minister has had these words addressed to him many times. People envy him his apparent assurance, and worry because they are beset with doubts. They wish they had faith of a greater quality or in greater quantity—whatever that might mean.

Sometimes we may find a new understanding of a word by considering what is its opposite. We usually find that people contrast faith with doubt—and in so doing, make their understanding of its meaning much more difficult. The author of the Epistle to the Hebrews properly contrasts faith not with doubt but with sight (Hebrews 11, 1–3). He calls it 'the evidence of things not seen'. No one who has faith has it without also having doubts. To realise the truth of this is to make us much less apprehensive of the degree of faith which is ours—when measured by us in inverse proportion to our doubts. This is an entirely false guide and the cause of much needless anxiety.

Now, where healing is concerned, we have to lay hold upon certain truths and hold them tenaciously, even when they are seemingly contradictory. So much of Christian truth comes to us in paradox.

We believe that God is good. We cannot therefore believe that He wills our suffering—though He certainly allows us to suffer. In the short term, in the immediate situation, in the overall context, God evidently allows us to suffer. This truth is often very difficult for Christians to accept. They prefer to believe that their suffering is their fault or because of their lack of faith. Both of these may be ingredients of their suffering. They are assuredly not sufficient wholly to account for it. In the case of our Lord Jesus Christ neither had any place at all. With no fault, and perfect faith, Christ went through Gethsemane to Golgotha. In so doing He wrought the world's salvation. It is far better to think that He was sent to His suffering, that He was sent to His crucifixion, than to think that the passion and cross were sent to Him.

As for Christ, so for the Christian. In the short term, in our immediate context, we are sent, sometimes called upon voluntarily to accept, sometimes unwillingly despatched, to pain and suffering. It is as if there were pockets of evil in the world which we are sent to deal with, as soldiers are sent into battle. In war there are casualties; some suffer and some may die. It will not be because God does not love us that this will happen. It will not be because we lack faith that we shall suffer. On the contrary, it may be just because we are, as it were, crack troops in His army that we shall be chosen for this role. Of course, God does not will us to suffer. The general who sends his troops into battle does not wish his men wounded or killed—but he allows that it may happen.

Here is the model, the analogy by which we may comprehend God's dealing with us. If we resent His call, if we refuse His commission or seek to evade it, we shall not deal effectively with the situations to which we are sent. We may only learn in such situations why we are there and what it is that we have to do. If we do learn it, we may ourselves grow increasingly in grace and spiritual stature. Of course we may still pray for deliverance, as a soldier may pray that a campaign may end before his endurance is further taxed. The paradox of joyful acceptance and unremitting prayer for deliverance is another expression of the truth which we have to learn.

We know that the problem of pain and suffering vexes the human mind and heart more than all others. It is in one sense insoluble. No one can, philosophically or theologically, provide a single answer that will solve the problem for ever and for everyone. The struggle to understand why some people have to suffer so much and for so long is an interminable one, but we engage in that struggle with certain beliefs. Armed with them, we begin to make some sense of what is happening. We perceive in it some purpose and some meaning. In so doing, we find some degree of peace of mind and some capacity for helping others. The beliefs we hold will often best be expressed, to ourselves and to other people, in the guise of models, metaphors or analogies. These will be based on the firm and sure assertions which Christians can and indeed must make. Among these assertions will be that of faith, in the love and the power of God. Whatever the situation, the Christian must never compromise his belief that God's love is absolute and His power greater than all the forces of evil. That he often doubts these facts he must not take to be lack of faith, but rather evidence of it. Faith is believing, against the immediate evidence, because of convictions based more profoundly and more surely than the immediate. It is not unreasonable; nor is it unscientific. If science or reason could disprove the grounds for faith, faith must at once be abandoned.

Sometimes faith is abandoned for quite other reasons. People say this or that happened and I lost my faith. Perhaps they never really had it; perhaps it was founded on altogether false premises. One sure thing is that the loss of faith or the lack of faith adds nothing to the reasonableness of anyone's approach to life, or to pain. It is difficult to believe—but much more difficult not to! For, not to believe means hiding oneself from a vast weight of evidence, from a great cloud of witnesses. But faith will always be accompanied by doubt and, for the Christian, only replaced by sight.

But what of miracles?

CHAPTER VI

Miracles

When we first proposed to hold healing services at St Marylebone Parish Church, one devout member of the congregation expressed her unease at the idea by asking if there was not a real danger that people might come expecting miracles. It would be a sad reflection indeed on the state of the health of the Church if it abandoned its expectation of miracles or came to regard that expectation as dangerous. In the next chapter we shall look more closely at expectations and see how they often need to be healed. But people do not need to be cured of an expectation of miracles—providing of course that we know what we mean when we use that word!

The average person would appear to require three ingredients in any event that he would want to describe as miraculous: that it should be inexplicable, that it should be immediate and that it should be spectacular. Sometimes one or all of these adjectives do apply, but not often and certainly not necessarily.

The word 'miracle' is derived from a Latin word which means 'to wonder at'. It has the same basic root as the word 'admire'. A miracle is therefore any event that causes us to wonder, or to 'admire' or to lift up our hearts to God, as Charles Wesley has it, 'lost in wonder, love and praise'. If the explanation of the event escapes us, it may seem to us all the more wonderful. If the explanation is later forthcoming, it should in no way detract from our admiration, from our worship of God—for indeed the Christian is meant to wonder at all God's activities. He singles out some in order that He may not fail to recognise all, as the objects of His wonder and the occasion of His worship. In the New Testament, we saw our Lord working miracles—many of them involving cures for the sick and some the restoration of life to the dead. How does the twentieth century Christian evaluate them?

First, we must recognise that, in an age where knowledge was so much less, the number of events which were inexplicable and therefore thought of as 'miraculous' was much greater than it would be today. But the real factor which gave our Lord's miracles the character they had, for those who witnessed them and for all of us who believe in them, was the factor of what is called 'divine intervention'. Did God, in Christ, and does God today, through human intermediaries or independently of them, 'intervene' in the course of events? The answer to that question depends upon what we mean by the 'course of events' and shows why this study began with an exposition of Creation. If God set the universe in motion a very long time ago, it would in any case be a strange judgment on His omnipotence if He had from time to time to intervene, to set the work right, to correct the 'course of events'. But if Creation did not take place millennia ago, but is going on now, if God *is* creating rather than *did* create, our understanding of miracles requires no such belief in 'intervention'. Miracles are the order of the day. Everything God does may make us wonder—but of course from the human perspective some things are more wonderful than others! But whether perceived by us as miraculous or not, everything that happens is simply what God is doing next. There never was, or could have been, a different course. The miracle is how *we* perceive God's activity, not how *He* does!

The Incarnation event was full of miracles. Human history is not even; it has periods of seeming ordinariness and dullness as well as periods of excitement, discovery and change. The Incarnate Life of Christ is, for the Christian, the most significant period in all history, so different from all others as to be described as indeed different in kind. It was a period best described as God recreating—not because He had got it wrong in the first place, but because by its nature it was 'due for renewal'. Every miracle that our Lord performed was in one sense explicable. The fact that those who witnessed them had not the knowledge to explain them is *not* the point that makes them miraculous. So today, God acts: that is His Nature. We understand very little. When things happen unexpectedly, especially in answer to prayer, we say 'MIRACLE!' Not that the seemingly ordinary events of life should be thought otherwise, but that all things in God's creative activity may call from us wonder and should lead to praise.

So do we believe in miracles of healing? Of course we do. Usually they will be occasioned by the skill of the physician or surgeon. Sometimes the petition or intercession of a Christian onlooker may be the final step in the process of recovery. But we need to assert most forcefully that it is not the immediacy or the spectacular element nor that it is inexplicable which makes the event a miracle. All these ingredients are rare and none is essential. Not only is that true but we shall surely be grateful that it is so. Accounts of sudden and spectacular healings are numerous, and are often—though not always—well authenticated. Rarely do we hear of what follows.

A woman in my experience was flown half across the globe for surgery for cancer. After prayer and the laying on of hands—done for her vicariously—she was completely free of all symptoms. She was left bewildered and deeply distressed as well as relieved by what had happened. The analogy with someone who wins a fortune on the football pools is apt. The euphoria of the sudden acquisition of undreamed of wealth is often followed by all sorts of problems which stem from the total disruption of life-style and the loss of a need to work. Assuming that to acquire wealth is a good thing, it is well to come by it gradually rather than suddenly—the same is equally true for health!

I once heard of a bishop who was offered a lift by a lorry driver. When he got into the cab the driver could not start the engine. After trying all the tricks he knew, he appealed to the

bishop to say a prayer. Somewhat reluctantly the bishop did—
and the lorry started. But it was the bishop who was surprised.
And rightly so, for that is not the normal way that engines are
made to work. Prayer is not designed to replace the work of the
mechanic anymore than it is of the surgeon. Prayer in such a
context would usually be for insight or perhaps for patience,
and fruits of prayer, no less than the occasional instant solution
to the problem, call for our wonder.

Miracles are the everyday life of the Church, if the Church
is true to itself. Individually and corporately we are to be for
ever regarding God as being 'in *all* His work most wonderful',
as well as 'most sure in all His ways'.

But what about expectations? This is a matter of major
importance so to that difficult subject we must now turn.

CHAPTER VII

EXPECTATIONS

At a Healing Service, the first thing that needs to be healed may well be the expectations of some at least of those who come. So it is with those who come to the priest or minister at a more personal level. 'Do you do healing?' 'Are you a Faith Healer?' 'Can you give me some healing?' These are natural and urgent questions. Always we have to answer that we do not know what God will do. All things are in His power, but He will not break His own rule. He will act and He will act characteristically. He will not say 'You should have come yesterday' or 'You must come again tomorrow'. His mercies are ever in fruit. All occasions invite them and all times are His seasons—but He knows and we do not know. He is omniscient and we are ignorant. We cannot tell what He will do for us until He Himself reveals it in what He does.

For the Christian the only proper expectations are to be thought of in this way. Urgently we may desire. Vigorously we may express that desire. We must make no assumptions except that God will be God, will be the Father of our Lord Jesus Christ. His ministers are to minister this truth as the first prerequisite of all healing. For no man is a healer—only God. We may mediate His gifts of healing; we may be instruments of His grace and channels of His power. He alone can determine what He will mediate through us.

Once this principle has been established, there are certain expectations which can be discounted and some which can be encouraged. Our Lord's miracles included not only the curing of the sick but also the raising of the dead—are we to believe that His ministers may ever reverse the process of dying? Some indeed have been called back from the brink of death and our understanding of what constitutes the moment or the event of death may be called in question by such case histories as that of Dorothy Kerin*. But there is no recorded example in Christian Healing of a calling forth from the tomb, such as our Lord Jesus Christ appears to have done for Lazarus, or to a resurrection from three days sleep in death such as He Himself is deemed to have experienced. Nor is there any record of an amputated leg growing again in consequence of prayer or sacrament. Neither patient or minister ever have such expectations. They are not among the options. We need not say that God could not. We do say that He does not act in that way. We shall not expect or ask Him to do so.

If there are medical conditions which are not susceptible to what we call Christian Healing, can we list those that are? We can go some way in doing so. First and foremost are the so-called psychosomatic diseases. The concept of physical illness being the expression of mental or spiritual ailments finds its parallel in the way in which Christians use sacraments. If physical outward, visible, tangible, audible signs can bring grace to the recipient of them, then physical symptoms occasioned by the lack of grace can be cured by its influx consequent upon prayer and sacrament. The sacramental principle is closely related to the psycho-somatic concept in medical diagnosis. We may have a patient with a heart condition. He goes to his doctor and to his cardiologist. His condition is not really one of disease but of stress and anxiety. The Churches' ministry is one in which he finds alleviation of that stress and his heart condition may be cured. Of course there will be other factors in his condition—known or unknown to the patient. His healing cannot therefore be guaranteed. But his expectation of healing is to be encouraged and in itself is a factor in his recovery.

Another patient has lost all incentive to get better. After

---

* See *Will you go back* by Ruth Farr, published by The Dorothy Kerin Trust, Burrswood. Dorothy Kerin was the founder of Burrswood, the Home of Healing at Groombridge in Kent.

successful surgery, she has nonetheless resigned her will to live and is slowly declining. Scientific medicine has no remedy to offer her. I knew a patient once whose condition was precisely that. The doctor asked the chaplain if he could help. He challenged the patient to list all her grievances but, having done so, to list her blessings too. She began the first list with her being in hospital and immediately recognised that it should properly be listed as a blessing. She began again, with the second list and marvelled at how much she had taken for granted. She resolved that if she recovered she would try to lead a life with more gratitude in it and so with more generous service to others. Her resolve was the occasion for beginning to recover and she did. The ministry of the Christian priest awakened in her a sense of gratitude and indebtedness to society which she knew she ought to repay. Her expectation had not so much to be cured as to be implanted.

Multiplication of such kinds of situations need not be made. There is obviously a vast area where expectation of recovery is to be encouraged and hope raised high. But it must be remembered that the Christian Ministry of Healing, though it may focus on a particular action, of prayer or sacrament or healing service, should always include the ministry of personal counselling and the option of being received into a warm and welcoming congregation. The patient who rejects any part of the total ministry of the Church may put his healing at risk just as the patient who takes only part of his prescribed medicine will do the same.

Then there are the many patients who come for Christian Healing whose sickness is evidently of the mind and its physical manifestation relatively unimportant. Can the Church relieve depression or cure schizophrenia? Her ministry of loving care and support may indeed bring relief of some of the symptoms and may impart the will to carry on and to live life as fully as possible. The will to carry on is properly speaking the great Christian virtue of hope. Hope is not mere optimism. People may be blessed with an optimistic temperament or seemingly cursed with a pessimistic one. But hope is a grace which all can have, and where it is not infused it can and should be acquired. It is right and important to encourage people to hope for whatever they want. If and when the object of that hope is disappointed, the attitude of hope will find a new object and ultimately one that cannot and will not be disappointed, God Himself. We shall hope for God more readily and not less if we have lively hope of His blessings on our journey.

It cannot be overstressed that the caring community of Christian people is of vital importance. The priest, the minister, lay people with spiritual gifts, may have a very great part to play in helping, in praying and in counselling. The enormous advantage they have over their medical counterparts is the offer of membership of the therapeutic community, the loving, caring, welcoming Church.

What of spiritual disease? Of recent years, this has been the only one brought to the ministry of the priest. I cannot pray; I am burdened with a sense of guilt or unworthiness. I have lost my faith. The expectation of cure of these maladies must be fostered and encouraged and means of help offered. Teaching and unteaching are often of great importance.

I ministered recently to a woman in hospital, taking her Holy Communion and talking to her over a period of some weeks. One day when I went in she told me she had just been told that she had an incurable cancer and her life expectation was weeks rather than months. 'All I have to look forward to is weeks of pain and now there is no light at the end of the tunnel.' I talked to her of the light Christians believe there will be at the end of that tunnel. The light of a welcoming father's face, a home-coming banquet, a robe and a ring. Do *you* really believe it? she asked. Do *you* never doubt? I told her that I often doubted but that nevertheless that belief was and must always be the guiding star in the life of every Christian. Start to look forward, start to hope. She died knowing.

Another woman to whom I ministered had no fear of death and no doubt about the after-life. But the thought of that after-life terrified her. How could she possibly expect to go to Heaven, considering the kind of life she had led? (It was in fact no worse than average, if no better.) The God she believed in was not the Father of our Lord Jesus Christ. He was the object of her fear not of her love. She had no hope of salvation, only a fear of damnation. Unlearning was more important for her than learning. But it was the same image of the loving father, painted for us by our Lord Himself, that began to persuade her that she too could look forward.

The unlearning of images of God, of the fear of hell, of the nature of guilt—this is healing indeed and a peaceful death, as opposed to an agonised one, the fruit of that healing.

Sometimes the question arises, what of those physical conditions which lie between the psycho-somatic stress and the amputated leg? Can cancer be cured by prayer? Can sight be restored by sacrament? The danger of false expectations in these areas is very considerable. But we know so little of all that there is to know about the vast number of conditions and it has been abundantly demonstrated that it may be the case that spiritual intervention is the missing factor and its supply may bring a physical remedy in highly unexpected areas.

Two dangers immediately occur: one is that the patient or his friends will take themselves to every 'healer' and agency that has ever made a claim to a cure. It is the quest for the 'magic wand'. Someone, somewhere has it, if only I can find him. In seeking it such people miss what God is offering as well as not finding what they seek.

The other danger is the loss of what God is trying to teach them, the blessing which God is actually trying to communicate to them. Countless patients have found God and have found peace and meaning for their existence only in the acceptance of pain and sickness and of death. By raising false expectations or encouraging false optimism, we do people no service, for they may forfeit blessings greater than life itself. The eternal things of God which go beyond life and death are the things of which eternity is made.

Let us look, then at what we should believe about the 'last things'.

CHAPTER VIII

'LAST THINGS'

In an earlier chapter we saw how a word or idea can often be better understood when we have considered what constitutes its opposite. We saw that faith is often contrasted with doubt. But its proper opposite is sight and the realisation of this enables a clearer comprehension of the true meaning of faith.

The word death is commonly contrasted with life and, in consequence, many false ideas surround our thoughts about it. Death is more properly contrasted with birth. They are both events. Both mark an end, in one sense, but much more importantly, a beginning. Death is the gate to life eternal. In the early church, at funerals, white not black was the liturgical colour. White was a token of joy and rejoicing; that a soul had entered Paradise. Mourning at a funeral in grief expresses our own physical loss. We have no occasion to weep for the departed but it often helps if we can shed tears for ourselves.

Nevertheless death is often thought of as defeat, as failure or even as a tragedy. Doctors and nurses are quite properly committed to the preservation of life. When they do not do so they regard their ministry as having failed. But the Christian believes that life is a preparation for death, and that for some people, ultimately for us all, dying will be our healing. Somebody once said that we are all suffering from an incurable disease called mortality. But it is not a disease and we should not suffer from it or because of it. If we know that it leads into another life our thinking about it is totally altered. It is of the greatest importance that we should believe rightly about the 'last things'—Heaven and Hell, Death and Judgment.

If Christian theology from the human point of view begins

with creation, so it must end with a consideration of our destiny. The analogy of life as a journey presupposes a destination. To travel purposefully and hopefully demands a concept of a goal towards which we are moving. We call it 'Heaven' and we build ourselves mental models to help us to focus on what it must be like.

The Scriptures, and the Church which must expound them and be faithful to their teaching, has likewise had a doctrine of Hell. Again we conceptualise it as if it were a place. It is the state of separation from God

> *To turn aside from Thee is Hell*
> *To walk with Thee is Heaven.*

It is the state of the damned as Heaven is the state of the blessed. But it is one of the greatest, if not the greatest, of theological problems to reconcile an eternal Hell, an everlasting damnation, with belief in an all-loving, all-merciful and all-purposeful God. Some of the problems are solved by belief in an intermediary state between earth and Heaven, which is sometimes called 'Paradise', a garden, and sometimes 'Purgatory', a place of cleansing. Not everyone realises that the two words refer to the same estate, one name having overtones of joy and the other of suffering. It has been suggested that both the joys and the sufferings of this intermediate condition are greater than those experienced on earth. Here we shall experience the joy of a journey ended, the joy of a 'welcome home', the joy of a glimpse of the vision of God. But that glimpse must also be painful, as it always hurts the eyes to come out of darkness into bright sunlight. The cleansing process is painful because of our recognition of the reality of sin, of our new awareness of God's love and the effect of our disobedience.

If not all the difficulties of the rejection of a belief in an eternal Hell are solved by a wholesome doctrine of Paradise, it is my contention that such a doctrine of Hell should still be rejected. Our ultimate belief in God, as the Father of our

Lord Jesus Christ, as being as He is in Jesus cannot sustain a belief that He could ultimately allow any of His children to be lost. Jesus said 'I, if I be lifted up, will draw all men unto me'. There is a universality in these words which is inconsistent with an eternal Hell or an everlasting damnation.

But what of Heaven? Of course it is not really a place. It is outside both time and space, a condition or estate. But it helps us to build an analogy with a place and need do us no harm so long as we remember that we are using the language of parable or metaphor. Heaven no more occupies space than do love, joy and peace, which are among its 'ingredients'.

Its principle 'ingredient' is God and we see it first as the place of our vision of Him. The Vision of God is man's *Summum Bonum*, his greatest good. Heaven is thus our home because it is where we see God, Who is our Father in Heaven. All our images of Heaven must be compatible with His pervasive presence and subordinate to it.

As we journey through life, we inevitably use physical, this-worldly analogies to make our pictures of Heaven, just as Jesus did in so many of His parables. Fred Astaire used to sing 'I'm in Heaven when I'm dancing cheek to cheek'. The worldly accomplishment which gave him the greatest happiness was a useful model for what eternity would be like for him. We may quite properly do likewise.

I remember once hearing a speech delivered by the priest under whom I served in my first curacy, Canon William Campling. He was Vicar of Roehampton, and years after he retired, he returned to make a presentation to the retiring organist. Roehampton had, and still has, a great musical tradition, and Canon Campling was by then very deaf. 'I cannot hear music now,' he said, 'I shall have to wait until I go to Heaven.' And then he added, 'I don't know if they use the *English Hymnal* there, but I know that if I want it I shall have it.' That was in fact a very profound theological statement. It matches Peter Abelard's great description of Heaven,

Wish and fulfilment shall severed be ne'er,
Nor the thing prayed for fall short of the prayer.

In Heaven we cannot want what we cannot have, for our wanting
and our having are both utterly dependent on God's will.

The best analogies of course will be chosen from the highest
plane of our temporal existence, the spiritual. On earth, because we are made up of the three component 'parts' of body,
mind and spirit, we experience joys at all these three levels.
We may call the joys of the body 'pleasures', those of the
mind 'happiness' and those of the spirit 'blessedness'.

Christianity has never been well served by Puritanism, which
is a denigration of the joys of the body and often an outright
condemnation of them. This is false. It is of course true, as
Robert Burns had it, that

> *Pleasures are like poppies spread,*
> *You seize the flower, its bloom is shed,*
> *Or like a snowfall in the river,*
> *A moment white, then melts for ever.*

Or partly true! For not all worldly physical pleasures are quite
so brief. All of them are transitory, but all of them still come
from God and are His creation and His gift. We are meant to
enjoy them and to give thanks for them. We must nevertheless
remember that they are more lowly in God's hierarchy than
happiness or blessedness.

The distinctions are of course to some extent artificial.
Just as we cannot ultimately separate our bodies, our minds
and our souls, because we are what they are and in their
interaction and their interrelationships, so pleasure, happiness
and blessedness merge into each other. But for the purpose
of analysis we can look at them separately, and it may help
to see happiness as belonging more to the mental level of
human life and experience. We are happy in our relationships with other people, in our appreciation of literature, of music or of art. We are happy in our work, in our

leisure activities. We are happy to enjoy good health. The objects of human happiness we naturally, normally and rightly, regard as being on a higher plane, and as being more praiseworthy and more worthwhile than the physical pleasures which are more particularly related to our senses. But they are still transitory and they belong to the passing things of time, and they cannot ultimately be ours.

Blessedness is therefore the highest in the hierarchy of human joy. It relates to the eternal things of God and the human spirit. Jesus Himself pronounced certain conditions to be blessed. We find His list of these at the beginning of His famous Sermon on the Mount, in the opening verses of St Matthew's Gospel, Chapter 5, the so-called Beatitudes.

So the Christian sees pleasure and happiness as belonging to the journey and to the journey only. They are things to be enjoyed, but not if they interfere with the progress of that journey, impede his way or divert him from it. Blessedness is not of course to be ours only hereafter, it is also ours on the journey. On the journey the condition of blessedness enables us to keep pleasure and happiness in perspective and in proportion. But the conditions of blessedness we also take with us; the world did not give them and the world cannot take them from us. They do not emanate from the transitoriness of life, and are not forfeited when life ends.

If Peter Abelard is to be followed, we recognise that in Heaven there is no separation between wish and fulfilment, and it follows that the Christian on pilgrimage is always endeavouring to wish what God would have him wish, to want what God wants for him, to love what He commands, and to desire what He promises.

This puts health and healing into their proper perspective. We seek healing as a means not as an end. We seek it in order that we may love, serve and worship God more fully. Holiness is the condition of worship, perfect holiness of perfect worship, realisable only in Heaven itself, but sought earnestly all through life's journey.

CHAPTER IX

WORSHIP

The last chapter ended with the assertion that we seek healing as a means and not as an end. It is often difficult to convey to the congregation at a healing service that we are there primarily to worship and not to seek healing. The effect of original sin is that man is for ever placing himself at the centre of his universe and usurping the place which is God's alone.

Arthur Christopher Benson, the Victorian Man of Letters, describes a traumatic and highly significant event in his young childhood. He recounts that as a little boy he went up to bed one summer evening, and after he had been asleep for a little while he was awakened by sounds reaching him through his bedroom window. He got up to look out and was greeted by the sight of his mother playing croquet with a group of her friends on the lawn beneath. He was deeply shocked by the sudden realisation that his mother did not exist merely as his personal appendage. She had a life of her own.

It is very easy to fall into the error of supposing that God exists for us. We need to be reminded that he has a life of His own. In an earlier chapter we referred to the value of the Christian Year. Through it we celebrate Sunday by Sunday the saving events of the Incarnate life of Christ—all the things He has done for us. We begin with looking forward to His birth; we end with His Ascension and His gift of His Holy Spirit. But then there is another Sunday. We call it Trinity Sunday and on it we celebrate who God is rather than what He has done. Nothing could be more important.

In our daily prayer and in all our public worship, not one Sunday in the year but always, worship and praise come first. They are not the means to any end. They are not done for a purpose. They are the ultimate end, the ultimate acts of loving.

Healing of course includes an understanding of God. We have said that He is as He is in Jesus. The incarnate life of our Lord tells us of His care and compassion, of His ultimate love for His children. He is perceived as a trinity of persons, a formula which has often demanded an explanation rather than been one. Certainly He is not a God of parts. Persons does not mean people. We perceive Him as our Father, our loving Creator, whom we can know and approach as a child does his father. We perceive Him in Jesus and see that our Lord was the express image of God's person. The Holy Spirit, who gives life to the Christian and to the Church itself, is God among us, our strength and our guide.

When St Augustine wrote his great treatise on the nature of God he had a vision. He saw a child on the sea shore who was scooping the sea water into a hole in the sand. He asked the child how he thought he could comprehend so much water in so small a hole. The child turned into an angel and asked him how he thought he could contain God in his little mind. Man has yet to understand fully the nature of one human cell. He does not understand himself. Still less does he understand God. But he has a duty to know what he can know, what God has revealed and what by his own reason inspired by the Spirit of God, he may learn. Ignorance of what can and should be known is itself sickness and leads to other maladies of heart and mind.

It has often been said that it doesn't matter what we believe so long as we do what is right. This is a great error. How can we possibly do what is right if we believe what is not true? Our activities stem from our thoughts and our belief. They are in constant need of healing. Conduct tests belief and the quality of our prayers. We are indeed known by our fruits. The spiritual remedies of prayer and worship are of great importance even though they are essential by-products of the activities which, as we have said, are done for their own sake and not for ulterior purposes.

Bible study too, is an end in itself. We do it primarily as an act of love for God. But it also affects our daily living—and makes our lives more pleasing to God. I told one woman that to read the Bible daily would change and affect her attitudes in every area of life. 'It sounds like brain washing,' she said— and that is exactly what it is. The pejorative overtones of that exclamation have of course no place in this context. The words here mean exactly what they say. The brain and the mind are cleansed by the effect on them of God's word just as the heart and feelings are.

The opening words of the Athanasian Creed are 'The catholic faith is this, that we worship'. It goes on to make assertions rather than explanations about the nature of God. But it makes the essential point that the Christian religion is ultimately about worship not works. Healing is about being fit for God—for His praise and His glory. Health is for God.

Part II

CHAPTER X

SOME OLD TESTAMENT MODELS

It was part of the genius of the Hebrew mind to tell stories. Old Testament theology is largely taught in the history of the nation and in the biographies of its people. I propose, in this chapter, to explore some Old Testament 'case histories'. They were written with suberb insight and they are valid for all time. The first I have chosen is the story of Jacob.*

JACOB

Jacob was the son of Isaac and the younger, twin, brother, of Esau. His story begins with his persuading his elder brother, in a moment of exhaustion and fatigue, to sell him his birthright in exchange for a bowl of soup. Later he impersonates Esau at his father's death-bed and robs him of the blessing due to the elder son. In consequence of this deception he flees home and goes to Haran, to his mother's brother Laban, for fear that Esau will kill him. On his journey he has his first recorded religious experience. He spends a night at Luz, afterwards called Bethel, and has a dream. He sees angels ascending and descending a ladder, which stands between earth and heaven. (Angels at the period and place when this story was written had not yet been thought of as possessing wings, so the ladder is not so surprising.) The Lord stands beside Jacob, reveals Himself to him, makes certain great promises concerning his destiny and evokes a response—albeit somewhat conditional—of dedication on his part.

* Genesis 27–32.

This event may indeed be thought of as Jacob's 'conversion'. He meets God, he hears God's gracious promises; he dedicates himself to His service. It is an experience without trauma; repentance is not called for nor confessed; no demands are made upon Jacob. He continues his journey and arrives at his uncle's home. He marries both of his cousins, Leah and Rachel. Many children are born to Leah and to his wives' slave girls; and ultimately Joseph is born of Rachel herself. He finally quarrels with his father-in-law and decides to return to his own country. He had come forth with nothing but his staff. Now he has two companies.

The reason he has divided his company into two is because he greatly fears meeting his brother Esau again. He sends his emissaries but they return to say that Esau is approaching him, without any indication of his disposition. Jacob therefore divides his company into two, in the hope that at least half of his party may escape his brother's vengeance, if revenge is indeed his intent.

Jacob then retires for the night and the story of this next encounter with God is vividly described. It was as if a man wrestled with him until day break. His agony of mind is to be understood most especially in terms of fear, of guilt and of self-identity. He is afraid. He has lost the security of his uncle's home and is about to meet the brother he has so much wronged. He remembers Esau's desire to kill him. He has no reason to think that he is anything but in danger of his life. He must also fear for his wives, his servants and his flock. His fear is fuelled by his guilt. No longer can he stand light-heartedly to his deceit and fraud, as he was able to do as a youth at Bethel. He knows he has greatly harmed his brother and his remorse overwhelms him. He knows too that he is at a great turning point in his life. Such a point is normal and natural in the lives of everybody when mid-life is reached. In Jacob's case, the crisis coincides with, or is occasioned by his return home. He looks back over his life; and he looks forward wondering who he is and what is to become of him. He wrestles with himself, with the spirit of God within him; so poignant is his agony that it seems to be like a physical wrestling match. Jacob will not give in. He does not know how to make his surrender to God. Perhaps the darkness affords him some protection. The dawn breaks, to rob him even of that. 'Tell me your name,' says the Angel, which in Hebrew thought is a call to surrender. Jacob surrenders his name and in so doing finds his true self. No longer is Jacob the supplanter, but Israel, the Prince of God. When he asks the name of his adversary it is of course denied him. But he receives God's blessing, the imprimatur upon his new surrendered state and his new identity. He has become his true self.

Charles Wesley wrote a hymn in honour of Jacob's wrestling at Peniel and redeems the story from its Old Testament setting to a Christian understanding of man's identity with God.*

> *Tis Love! 'tis Love! thou diedst for me!*
> *I hear thy whisper in my heart!*
> *The morning breaks, the shadows flee;*
> *Pure universal Love thou art:*
> *To me, to all, thy mercies move;*
> *Thy nature and thy Name is Love.*

In our surrender to God, and through our Lord Jesus Christ, we do indeed discover His name; we discover it to be Love, demonstrated for ever in the life and passion, death and resurrection, not of God's angel but of His Son.

In the process of his spiritual wrestling, Jacob was physically wounded. We read that the Angel 'struck him in the hollow of his thigh', so that Jacob's hip was dislocated. We do not know if or when that wound was healed. Jacob would have regarded it rather as St Francis of Assissi did the stigmata—as a mark of God's love and favour. If he was never healed *of* it, he would say that he had been healed *through* it or *by* it.

The story of Jacob is one of the most profound in the Old

* 'Come O thou traveller unknown', Ancient & Modern Revised, hymn 343.

Testament. It does not neatly fit into the categories of modern case-work and still less of medical practice. But it distils for us the most profound of all of the considerations that we need to make, for ourselves and for others, about the nature of sin and guilt and its attendant fear; about the way God leads us from the simple to the profound experience of Himself, about how some physical pain at least may be viewed and about the soul's search for identity and meaning in the loving purpose of God.

BALAAM

My next case history is that of Balaam in the Book of Numbers*, a story less well known and on a superficial reading containing somewhat ridiculous associations. The story relates to the Exodus, to the progress of the Children of Israel from Egypt to the Promised Land. They are encamped in the lowlands of Moab on the farther side of the Jordan from Jericho. Balak, the King of Moab, is, with his people, terrified at the sight of the Israelite people and painfully aware of their capacity to destroy them 'as a bull licks the spring grass'. Not having the physical resources to defeat the Israelites in battle, he calls upon Balaam who has the power to bless and to curse, to come and denounce them. Balaam invites Balak's emissaries to stay the night while he waits upon God's word. God immediately forbids Balaam to go back with them to Balak or to curse the people 'because they are blessed'. The message is simple and direct and Balaam conveys it to the messengers. There the matter should have ended, but it did not. Balak is unwilling to be put off; he sends another ambassage with the promise of greater reward and an instant demand that Balaam should come and do his bidding. Balaam, though repeating his insistence that he can only do what God bids him, nevertheless invites them to stay while he learns 'what more the Lord has to say to

* Numbers 22–24.

me'. God apparently gives him leave to go down with the messengers but only to do what He tells him. Balaam evidently travels only with his own servants, and on the way, God demonstrates his anger with him by causing his ass to sink to the ground beneath him. The ass sees God's angel with a drawn sword standing in the way—a sight concealed from Balaam who is merely exasperated by the ass's behaviour. He strikes the ass; the ass addresses Balaam and demands an explanation of his cruel and angry behaviour. Balaam replies that he regrets having no sword to slay him with, when the Lord opens his eyes and he sees the angel and the cause of the ass's behaviour. He repents of all that he has done; repents of being on the journey at all, from which he offers to turn back. He is bidden to continue but only to do God's bidding. On arrival he frustrates the wishes of the King. Despite many offerings of sacrifice, from differing vantage points, always it is the same answer: 'What the Lord speaks to me, that will I say.' And the Lord spoke blessings and not curses.

Superficially the story seems one of gross injustice in which Balaam is punished despite his obedience and one of ridiculous nonsense in which an ass speaks with a human voice. Wherein then lies its value? The story is one of profound psychological insight and spiritual depth.

Balaam's first response to the messenger is plainly to tell them what God has made plain to him. His second response is quite different. He is no longer seeking to know God's will, for he knows it already. He is seeking to get it changed! So vividly written is Hebrew scripture that we sometimes forget that Balaam heard the voice of God in precisely the same way that we do; through prayer and waiting upon Him. He does not see God with a physical eye or hear his voice with a physical ear. His spirit is tuned to the Spirit of God, and in pureness of heart he knows God's will. On the arrival of the second messengers his heart is not so pure. With fear of the King's displeasure, coupled with greed for the reward and honour that are offered to him, he hopes to hear a different word and still pretend that it is God's. He convinces himself that he may go with the messengers so long as he resolves to say only what God bids him. He blinds himself to the fact that the journey has no possible point since its purpose is to evoke a curse and he can only speak a blessing. He deliberately allows himself to be led into temptation assuring himself that when the time comes, he will be able to resist. On the journey his conscience overwhelms him. What is he doing on the journey? The voice of the ass is the voice of his conscience. He hides himself from the angel of God's presence for he knows that in this context, the angel holds a sword against him. The seemingly ridiculous element in the story is its most profound. Just as Jacob had wrestled in his heart with God, so also Balaam. His cupidity is rebuked and his prevarication judged. And how does he respond? He longs to turn back, to escape and return to his state of innocence and, in the story, offers to do so. But he cannot. God bids him continue because to this there is spiritually no alternative. Repentance is never a return or a reversal. Sin may be forgiven but its effects can rarely be erased. We cannot become again as if we had not sinned. There is no turning back. Balaam had to go on. And he did. Even though he was still not wholly free from temptation, he was on the way to a deeper recognition of the unchangeableness of God's will. In the presence of Balak, it may have been more from fear than from self-seeking that he agreed to go on, looking for a place where he could do the King's bidding. But ultimately he overcame both temptations. He resorted no more to divination nor to prevarication. He allowed the Spirit of God to come upon him and uttered the oracle of blessing. Balaam was healed and made whole, and at last could simply 'go home'. He had found his peace.

So we learn that our peace lies in obedience to God's will. If He makes His way plain before our face, let us rejoice and walk in it, unswerved by worldly consideration. If we err, then we know that God's providence, though not letting us return, can still lead us on. It will be more painful because of our failure but it will be no less sure. He will not say, 'Because you should not be here, I cannot now lead you.' He will not say, 'You should have asked me yesterday and so now you must wait until tomorrow'. The moments of our sin if they are also the moments of our penitence are the moments of His mercy too. 'All occasions invite his mercies and all times are his seasons.'*

But God hath made no decree to distinguish the seasons of his mercies; in paradise, the fruits were ripe, the first minute, and in heaven it is alwaies Autumne, his mercies are ever in their maturity. We ask *panem quotidianum*, our daily bread, and God never sayes you should have come yesterday, he never sayes you must come againe tomorrow, but *to day if you will heare his voice*, to day he will heare you. If some King of the earth have so large an extent of Dominion, in North, and South, as that he hath Winter and Summer together in his Dominions, so large an extent East and West, as that he hath day and night together in his Dominions, much more hath God mercy and judgement together. He brought light out of darknesse, not out of a lesser light; He can bring thy Summer out of Winter, though thou have no Spring; though in the waves of fortune, or understanding, or conscience, thou have been benighted till now, wintred and frozen, clouded and eclypsed, damped and benummed, smothered and stupified till now, now God comes to thee, not as in the dawning of the day, not as in the bud of the spring, but as the Sun at noon to illustrate all shadowes, as the sheaves in harvest, to fill all penuries. All occasions invite his mercies, and all times are his seasons.*

JOB

My third Old Testament biography is that of Job. Of all the Old Testament books, none addresses itself more specifically

* Donne's Sermons: Selected Passages, Logan Pearsall Smith, Clarendon Press, p. 139.

to the problem of pain than does this. It gives us no direct answer, for no such response is, or ever will be, forthcoming, but it helps us in our own struggle to understand and to come to terms with suffering.

The story begins with an account of Job's righteousness and prosperity—in the eyes of the Hebrew writer the one was an invariable sign of the other. Satan is then seen taunting God, because Job, he says, serves God only because he has been so richly blessed. His service is all self-interest. He does not serve God for nothing. Deprived of His favour, he will curse God rather than bless Him. God agrees that Job should be put to the test and one tragedy after another besets him. He is stripped of everything. But his response to all his calamities is exemplary in the extreme, 'If we accept good from God, shall we not accept evil?' Throughout all this Job did not offer one sinful word.

The first chapter ends with the arrival of Job's three friends, who, despite the marvellous restraint of their initial encounter—for seven days they sat with him in silence—were soon to start their censorious and sanctimonious recrimination and drive him to the brink of despair. Speech after speech is uttered and replied to. A fourth friend appears to add fuel to the flames. Then God Himself answers. He makes no explanation. He merely observes upon the infinity of His own wisdom and knowledge and the limitation of Job's. In a hundred images He observes upon Job's littleness and His own greatness. And Job understands the impossibility of understanding. He recognises that patient faith and trust, not explanation and comprehension, are what are required of him. At this moment he is healed, not because his trials are less but because he now *sees* God, of whom before he had only *heard*. He repents not so much in the usual sense of acknowledging a sin, but in the sense of recognising that what he needed was trust, because he could not know, and this he now is able to do.

Perhaps the most moving verse in the whole story then follows: 'The Lord showed favour to Job when he interceded for his friends.' No greater mark of his healing could possibly be evidence. His natural desire for vengeance and recrimination was turned into a supernatural prayer for those who had persecuted him. That Job's physical fortunes were restored is a typical Hebrew commentary on his restoration to favour with God, an outward and visible sign of it. It is not often so, and never necessarily so. Job indeed came to learn that prosperity is not necessarily a mark of God's favour. Often it is those whom He loves most, if we can so speak of God, who are called to a life of privation and suffering. Job knew instinctively that a quiet acceptance of his sad lot was not the way to please God. It was in the very process of his struggle and argument that he came to know God and in the end to have His blessing.

We are not wrong 'to curse the day of our birth'. God would *not* have us disguise our feelings and our reactions or seek to hide from Him our pain. It is as we reveal them that they are interpreted and made meaningful. If they are not cured by such a process, still *we* are healed. In our relationship with those around us, with our family or our friends, we may often encounter lack of understanding and often hostility. We may react at the human level with anger and annoyance.

The story of Job teaches us that we may come through it to a love for them which shows itself in prayer; a prayer which may well have as its first fruit a blessing for us though that must not be the object of our doing it.

CHAPTER XI

SOME NEW TESTAMENT MODELS

Christian theology is partly founded upon the Hebrew genius for telling stories. Our Lord's own parables are the supreme example. His miracles of healing are not being called in question by treating them as enacted parables and, for us, as learning occasions.

THE PRODIGAL SON

The Parable of the Prodigal Son has been commented on in written word and spoken address countless thousands of times. What are its lessons for those who seek from it guidance for their work of Christian Healing?

It is not well called, despite the universal popularity of its title, the Parable of the Prodigal Son. Two sons feature in the story, but it is essentially a story about their father—and ours. It is a story about the nature of God, about the way He loves and treats His children, about the appropriateness of the response that He makes to their behaviour.

First we learn that God's pardon precedes our penitence and in a very real sense enables and occasions it. God does not wait for our repentance, He is always beholding us in the 'far-off-ness' of our sinful situation, with the eyes of love and mercy, with what the theologians call 'prevenient grace'. That is the nature of the God who made us, who holds us in life and awaits us at death. The sinner may be sure of his reception at his Father's hand. The dying find their greatest comfort in their realisation not of where they are going but to whom they are going. Nothing, no seeming evidence to the contrary, however powerful that evidence may sometimes be, must ever shake that axiom of our faith, that God is a God of love and mercy, who can and does forgive the greatest of sins, who can and does welcome home the worst of sinners.

The prodigal son experiences not less than his expectations, but more! He might genuinely hope to be treated as a hired servant. How does he cope with being treated so royally as a son? He might have expected food to fend off his hunger—but not the fatted calf. Perhaps God ensures that we do not presume upon His mercy by counting upon such treatment. But our Lord would assume that such is the nature of our Heavenly Father.

Notice too the motives of the prodigal son. It is his hunger that drives him to return home. It is the thought of the food that his father's servants have beyond their need that fills him with hope. But he thinks better of phrasing his encounter so! He will rather confess that he has sinned. What immense spiritual insight our Lord shows in His understanding of human motivation. That is what we are like! Mixed indeed in our motives. Not so much sorry as hungry! But what comfort and consolation it brings that even so we shall be acceptable, even so we shall have a robe placed upon our shoulders and a ring put on our finger.

I sometimes wonder what happened on the morning after the feast! Of course there was the reckoning, 'We will meet in my study after breakfast.' Forgiveness is not in that sense unconditional. It requires rehabilitation, amendment and a new purpose. But in God's order of events those things come afterwards and against the assurance of love and mercy bountifully bestowed. For if God's mercy were to depend upon our penitence and our amendment, the Incarnation would not yet have taken place! It was 'while we were yet sinners'* that Christ came and it is the fact of His coming that incites us to repentance.

---

* Romans 5, 8.

THE GOOD SAMARITAN

The Parable of the Good Samaritan is likewise something of a misnomer! It is not so much a story about him as about the man who fell among the thieves. Of course we want to identify with the Good Samaritan—and not with those who pass by on the other side. There is an evident lesson to be learnt in terms of service to our fellow beings in time of especial need and irrespective of colour, class or creed. But the question that our Lord posed to His questioner was 'Which of these three was neighbour?' His hearers were to identify with the man who has fallen into the hands of robbers. It is foremostly with him, then, that we are to identify. We are to see ourselves as help-less, as the victims of the evil violence of others, and perhaps of our own foolish recklessness too. We are to see whence help is not forthcoming and then to find that Christ is our neigh-bour, either directly or through some other agent, and that He alone can care for and cure us.

The parable is about a sick and wounded man and about the compassion that God has for him, represented by the Good Samaritan.

TWO MIRACLES

From two parables let us then turn now to two miracles of healing, both to be found in the 7th chapter of St Mark's Gospel. Their juxtaposition in Scripture serves to emphasise the considerable difference between the two events. All miracles of healing can of course serve as models for us, and, indeed, case histories! I select two merely to illustrate some of the important elements in our Lord's—and so in the Church's—approach to healing.

The first is the healing of the Syrophoenician woman's daughter. In the terms in which the story is told, it is an exorcism.

First we notice that the event took place in Gentile country and our Lord appears ready to go into the house of a non-Jew—a fact omitted from St Matthew's version! Racial prejudice was as rife in New Testament times as it is now and it was the Semites who were anti-Gentile rather than the other way round. Our Lord's action is a clear rebuke to such an attitude and a reminder to us that healing has to do with the healing of such divisions just as much as it has to do with the relief of an individual's physical symptoms. No one can be healthy unless he is healthily related to his environment. But to be healthily related to an unhealthy environment is to be unhealthy. Hence, of course, the Crucifixion. Our Lord could not retain His integrity and be in harmony with His environment, so He went to the death that that evil environment prescribed for Him.

In the story of His visit to Tyre and Sidon we see His breaking the convention of the apartheid of His day. As the story proceeds we may discern a playful dismissal of its tenets. His conversation with the woman who seeks His help suggests at first the dismissal of her plea on racial grounds. A more profound study suggests that though perforce His mission and ministry are restricted by time and space, as it must perforce have been for Him to be able to operate at all, yet those constrictions were not of principle but of practice; they could and would be broken if need arose. He breaks them here; with good humour He accepted not only the prayer but also the person of the Gentile woman, and He healed her daughter. It may well be that the true focus of the healing was in the acceptance of the mother. Whatever unclean spirit may have seemed to possess the daughter, we cannot doubt that the relationship between the two would have been vitiated by the mother's unhappiness, occasioned by her own feeling of rejection. She now finds herself accepted. She returns to her daughter changed and transformed by her encounter with Jesus. Would that not have been immediately reflected in the way she now meets her child and account for the devil having gone?

Those who wish to personify the devil and make more of the possession of the daughter by such a spirit of evil, may not be satisfied by this explanation. The casting out of evil spirits, on the supposition that those spirits have as it were a life of their own, leave a question usually unasked as well as unanswered: where has the devil gone? To possess another human soul? To its own place? The latter phrase, sometimes used by those who practise exorcism, tends to a dualism abhorrent to the Christian mind. Is there a 'place' that belongs to the devil outside the territory of God and the Kingdom of Christ? The answer must be 'No'.

Our Lord journeyed from Tyre to the Sea of Galilee where He performed a miracle of healing in very different circumstances. In the first story, the patient, if it was indeed the daughter and not her mother, was not so much as seen let alone touched. The healing was in and through her mother. On this occasion the deaf-mute was physically brought into the presence of Jesus, who performed certain 'sacramental' actions—outward and visible signs.

First let us notice that we can bring to our Lord for healing those who are in need in either of these two ways—by making petition in their absence or by bringing them physically. If we are near to them physically or emotionally, we may well be involved ourselves in the healing that follows and may indeed ourselves be in greater need than the evident patient. Secondly we notice that although our Lord is not constricted by the physical absence of the person for whom healing is sought, if the patient is present He may well use outward and visible signs as the means by which He performs His healing and as evidence to those who witness the event that the healing does indeed emanate from Him. What He did in the flesh, we should still do in and through His Church, by prayer and sacrament.

Finally in the latter story we are told that before our Lord healed the man 'He sighed'. What is the significance of that? It may well be that our Lord was asking Himself the question

'What will this man do with his new-found gifts of speech and hearing? Will he use them to the glory of God or in the pursuit of selfish gain or in the furtherance of some evil cause?' It is of the utmost importance that Christian healing should always include this challenging question, 'Made fit for what?' If a person has used his sickness and infirmity to the glory of God, then at least there is a likelihood that he will use his restored health likewise. Before anyone can or should look for healing, they should have studied to dedicate their sickness to God's glory. If remission of sickness is granted to anyone, he cannot regard himself as well unless he has likewise dedicated his health to the service of God and his fellow men. Health *is* for God.

Suppose that Adolf Hitler had been admitted to hospital for surgery in the 1930's; suppose that the ministration of all who tended him had been successful and the day came when he was to be discharged and pronounced fit. But who is to ask the question, fit for what? Who could possibly call a man fit who was fit only for the destruction of millions of his fellow-men in gas chambers and in a bloody war?

Christian healing evidently demands that the question, 'Fit for what?', be asked and answered. The answer clearly demonstrates that health and holiness are ultimately inseparable, for the answer is, fit for God, in loving relationship with Him and fit for His purposes.

CHAPTER XII

THE INGREDIENTS OF CHRISTIAN COUNSELLING

Among the many divisions occasioned by the growing apart of the medical and clerical professions is that between Counselling and Pastoralia. The clergy of the Church have always been expected to be pastors to their people. The distinguishing mark of the bishop is his shepherd's crook. His ministry is modelled upon the image of Christ, the Good Shepherd. In the confessional, the penitent seeks not only penance and absolution, but also counsel and advice. Where the formality of the confessional is not the norm, the relationship of the priest or minister to his people has always been seen in terms of pastoral care—indeed he often speaks of his people as 'his flock'. He does not of course think of them only collectively. A shepherd knows each of his sheep 'by name'.

Alongside the ministry of the Church, the medical profession has developed its own ancillary in what is usually called case-work. With the insights learned from the study of psychology and sociology, case-workers and counsellors have become professionals in their own right and have often made the pastoral care of the clergy seem amateur.

As the rift between doctor and priest is healed, so the insights of the social worker become more readily available to the priest. Nor is the traffic only in one direction. Each has something to learn from the other. The rapport may begin with the learning of each other's language and the understanding of each other's basic concepts.

The furtherance of this coming together has been greatly helped by the work of the Institute of Religion and Medicine.

Founded by Michael Ramsey, when Archbishop of Canterbury, it brings doctors and clergy together with their ancillary colleagues in local field groups, to share each other's concerns. It also works at a more academic level. In recent years doctors and clergy have studied and written about the common ground between them and explored in some depth the interface between religion and medicine. A major contribution of the late Dr Lambourne, psychiatrist and theologian, was the founding of the Diploma in Pastoral Studies at Birmingham University, where students from both the medical and theological disciplines come together in pursuit of this end.

Despite the undoubted progress and the joy that the drift is in the right direction, it has to be acknowledged that there is a great discrepancy of skill and capacity in both the medical and clerical professions. Some doctors and some priests are virtually without counselling skills, would make no pretence to have them, may even despise them—yet despite this limitation may remain in other respects good doctors and good priests.

The medical profession has however at its disposal, in hospital and in general practice, the assistance, when the doctor needs to call upon it, of the trained social worker. The clergy are less well organised. They recognise their need to be available to give help and pastoral care to the individual members of their flock. Some few have dedicated their whole life's ministry to the direction of souls and have brought not only healing but holiness too, to those who have turned to them for help. Others have sought to improve their pastoral skills by benefiting from the insights of the other professions and undergoing in-service training or sabbatical post-graduate study. In consequence, some clergy are thought of as 'Christian Counsellors' and some churches as agencies of this ministry.

It may be asked, what expectation of difference would there be between a secular counsellor and a specifically Christian one? The Christian counsellor must not be less professional than his secular counterpart. He ought to be expected to have all that the other has, and more too. The 'more' will not only be an added dimension but an enhancement of all the others. Let us examine this further by looking at some of the basic principles of counselling, and seeing in what way the Christian faith of the counsellor makes this difference.

The counsellor is taught the importance of 'Acceptance'. He learns that, as a principle of action, he must deal with his client as he really is. This does not of course mean approval, but it does mean acknowledging the reality of the situation and accepting the client accordingly. He knew that if the client is or feels rejected—and he may come expecting and even inviting that reaction—that will at best add to the client's malaise and at worst result in the breakdown of the relationship almost as soon as it has begun.

The Christian counsellor accepts all this. But he also perceives that his client is a fellow human being, made like himself, in the image of God. His worth, his value, is inalienable and the counsellor perceives his value as an agent of healing and a means of restoring the distorted image of the human nature which is also divine. The case-worker thus has to make himself acceptable to his client as a step in making the client acceptable to himself. He does so because he knows that God accepts all His children just as they are and that that common fatherhood makes all men his brethren.

He also remembers that our Lord accepted the most rejected people in the society to which he came—befriended them, suffered because of His concern for them.

There are of course, for the secular counsellor and for the Christian, many difficulties; in all of them the Christian is assisted by his faith and commitment. First, the counsellor must recognise as an obstacle the non-acceptance of something in himself. The Christian knows that though he must seek to come to terms with this, God already accepts him. He is then helped to accept the unacceptable in others.

The counsellor knows the danger of imputing to the client his own feelings and so assuming that he actually knows how the client is feeling. The Christian perception of the absolute uniqueness of every human being helps him to guard against this.

The counsellor is aware that he like all men may be guilty of bias and prejudice. The Christian often starts in his client's eyes at a disadvantage because he may be assumed to have such prejudice! It is sadly true that many people have distorted ideas of the convictions upon which Christian work is based and assume them to be or likely to lead to prejudice. No doubt, too, they often are and do. But the faith of the Christian ought to be an antidote to bias. His creed should help him to know and understand the creeds of others. His culture he knows to be one among many that God has created. He therefore respects his client even against the client's rejection of himself, whichever his background and encumbrances may be. He treats him as a unique individual. He knows him 'by name', as God knows all His children by name. He will show it by using it.

Acceptance carries with it an attitude to the client which must never be seen as judgmental. The secular counsellor knows this. He is not there to determine guilt or innocence; he is there to identify need. The Victorian concept of the 'deserving poor' has no place in his vocabulary. Worthiness is irrelevant. He is there to help, not to punish or to blame, nor indeed to praise! He knows how often his client will have come from an environment in which he may have received moral criticism. He also knows that the client's gross failure to live by the standard and norms of society does not necessarily mean that he does not accept or value these standards. Often he longs to have them reinforced and seeks help to enable him to live up to them.

The Christian counsellor adds to these perceptions his knowledge that 'God's power is shown chiefly in mercy and pity.' He knows that there is a sense in which God is our judge. He knows also that there is no sense in which he is. He knows that God's judgment is not vindictive but reaches out to achieve the reconciliation of those who err. He knows that despite the seeming evidence to the contrary, that God is a God of love and compassion. He knows that all Christians are called by the fact of their discipleship to exercise those graces—and none more so than those who are called to serve in the rightly-called caring professions.

It is important to lay hold upon the nature of God's judgment upon which the Christian Ethic is based. I once had an interesting dispute with a secular social worker. He was a Marriage Guidance Counsellor and after a lecture on the work of that excellent organisation, he was asked, 'Does the counsellor ever moralise?' An immediate and emphatic, 'No' greeted the question. But then he added, 'Of course, the counsellor may observe upon the logical consequences of the choices that people make.' He was taken aback when asked what he thought was the difference between that and moralising. Strictly speaking there is none. A Christian moralises, or explains the Christian Ethic solely in terms of consequence! Judgment, properly understood, is the logical consequence of the choices we make. So the Christian counsellor does not himself judge. He knows that he too is under judgment—having to live with the consequence of the exercise of his own free will.

The counsellor is taught the importance of client self-determination. It was Oscar Wilde who observed that though bad advice is always bad, good advice is absolutely disastrous! It robs the client of his capacity for making his own decisions, of accepting responsibility for his own life. The Christian counsellor can go on to say that every man is made in the image of God, that his freedom of choice is his most God-like possession; he can show how God longs to renew that image in him and to restore to him the supreme dignity of being human. His advice as a counsellor will only be to draw the attention of his client to the saving words and works of Christ and help him then to work out his own healing and salvation.

The Christian recognises that just as God does not destroy an individual's right to go his own way, however deleterious that way may appear to be, so he must resist any temptation to take charge of his client for his own good, to persuade him against his own judgment or to manipulate him or his situation to bring about what he, rather than the client, thinks should happen.

The counsellor is taught to beware of his own emotional involvement. If he has no compassion, he will be useless to his client. If he becomes over involved, he will quickly forfeit his capacity to help. He knows that what his client presents to him will be both *facts* and *feelings*. Everyone's problem is the sum of the objective reality and the subjective thoughts and feelings about that reality. Even if the objective reality is not a reality but something entirely imaginary, the subjective response remains the same and in itself entirely real. The case-worker seeks to make an appropriate response both to the facts and to the feelings about them. He tries to express that response only in so far as that expression will help his client to know and achieve his purposes. The Christian counsellor seeks to interpret the facts in a way consonant with God's activity in human history. What is God saying in this situation?

He also exercises the compassion of Christ and shows his own, as part of that fellowship in Christ's own sufferings in which both he and his client share. He does not therefore bear the client's suffering alone; he does so in fellowship and partnership with his Lord. He seeks to help his client to do the same. He will help the client to express his feelings to the degree which is appropriate, not only to himself but also to God.

The anger and the bitterness and the hostility which may overcome the client and may at times need to find an outlet, the counsellor must be ready to accept. But the Christian counsellor will help him to direct his feelings however hostile to God Himself. He will show that God is the source of all comfort, that His shoulders are broad enough to accept and His heart wide enough to forgive all the hostility in the world.

The counsellor is taught to be confidential. He must be trusted with the confidences of the client. The Christian counsellor knows that God Himself is privy to all that has been exchanged and binds the confidences with the seal of the confessional—to betray the client is to betray Christ Himself.

The counsellor has the temporal welfare of his client as his first consideration. He seeks to enable the client to return to his environment and then to live with a sufficient degree of usefulness and contentment. The Christian counsellor has that end in view too; but he asks a more ultimate question. To what purpose this temporal welfare? Is not this life a journey? How can a man be fit if he does not know what he is fit for? So he must seek to be fit for God and His glory. Fit to be a useful member of society. Yes, to be happy and content within himself; but also to be fit for God, fit for the advancement of His Kingdom. A man who has no sense of his ultimate purpose and destiny is not, in the Christian sense, well at all.

So the Christian counsellor not only adds God to the relationship of his client; he sees God in all the others and interprets them accordingly. It will be as natural and normal for him to pray with and for his client as it is to talk to him himself. This does not of course mean that he will always do so. The client may have no such desire, may be angry or embarrassed by the suggestion. The Christian counsellor must ever seek to be sensitive to what at any given moment, with any particular person, is apt and appropriate and so his Christian faith and conviction must only become explicit when it will help the client for them to do so.

CHAPTER XIII

THE INGREDIENTS OF
THE HEALING SERVICE

To the question, 'Do you hold Healing Services in your Church?' the strictly accurate answer should be, 'Yes; all our services are healing services.' Whenever the Word of the Lord is proclaimed and heeded, wherever the Sacraments are administered and received in faith, healing takes place, people are changed and the Kingdom of God is enlarged.

The purpose of all acts of worship is to give glory to God and to extend His Kingdom; people are changed in the process of worship in order that this fundamental purpose may be realised. Healing is not for its own sake; it comes as a by-product of giving praise to God and it comes that we may be enabled the better to praise Him.

Is Baptism then a Healing event? Evidently and supremely so. For in Baptism we proclaim the healing and saving acts of our Lord and lay claim upon His promise—for ourselves and on behalf of those who are candidates, be they infants or adults.

The Eucharist we have already explored in this context. In Holy Communion the grace of God given in Baptism is constantly renewed, 'until His coming again', as we are born into the church at the font so at the altar our life is sustained by the bread and the wine, the symbols of Christ nurturing both our bodies and souls.

Having recognised then that all services are about healing it is nevertheless the fact that healing services are generally taken to mean occasions of worship where the specific emphasis is on the healing in mind, body or spirit, of those who come. It may be an anointing or the laying on of hands, either in the context of Holy Communion, or as an appendage to the office of Morning or Evening prayer. It may be in a rite especially devised for the occasion.

Some would say that the ministry of healing should always be in the context of the Eucharist and there are strong theological grounds for supporting that contention. The Coronation Rite was once described as a 'Eucharist at which a monarch happens to get crowned'. But there are powerful reasons too for a specially devised service. Among the foremost of these is that the greater sacrament tends to dwarf the lesser and to reduce its impact and importance. It has also to be recognised that many who come to a healing service are outside the eucharistic congregation and would have little or no idea of what it is about. Furthermore, the specially constructed rite can be so much more evidently ecumenical than the Service of Holy Communion of a particular denomination.

Let us look at how such a rite should be constructed. If it is to include both anointing and laying on of hands, explanation must be made of the difference between them. The generally accepted view is that anointing is administered only after due preparation and with the opportunity of follow-up counselling. It is only administered once for the same condition. Those who come for the laying on of hands may do so for the renewal of grace that is given in Holy Unction, or independently of it; they may come frequently, making only their own preparation; they may have no wish, no need, and perhaps no opportunity to tell the minister of the particular need they bring.

At every service of the Church, there is always the Ministry of the Word—scripture reading(s) and usually an exposition in the form of a sermon or address. At a healing service, the lessons and the address are of the highest importance. Whatever else is left unsaid, the expectations of those who come must be addressed. These may need to be redirected. I have already said that the first thing that may need to be healed at a Healing Service are the expectations of those who come. A

Healing Service can easily be an occasion for sorrow or disappointment if considerable responsibility is not exercised. Whenever a service has a special intention, that which makes it special must be carefully considered and addressed. The readings at a Healing Service and the sermon which expounds them must touch the hearts and minds of the hearers; they must meet their need; they must teach them what they do not know, or have forgotten; they must bring comfort and encouragement; they must often challenge; they must bring forth thanksgiving and praise. Obviously they cannot always do all these things for all the people present. But that must always be the aim.

Since a Healing Service is always an emotive occasion, care must be taken not to arouse emotions unnecessarily or gratuitously. An atmosphere of peace and of reverent dignity throughout is all important. Music, which is itself a very healing thing, must be chosen to conduce to this end, the hymns too must be selected with the same purpose in view. If they are of a subjective nature, added vigilance is necessary.

An examination of the Order of Service* will show that it is prefaced with an Introduction or Welcome. This will always include some explanation of the procedures to those who are present for the first time. They will be told that all may come to receive the laying on of hands—the 'well' and the 'sick' alike—for in fact none of us are really well and all of us have needs. They will be told not to seek out a particular minister at the altar rail (if more than one is ministering) since all are equally channels of God's grace and none more so than another; the logistics of coming forward and returning will also be explained. They will be invited to meet each other after the service and told too that if they wish for a follow-up interview, then is the time to ask for it (and it must always be available).

The service begins with an Acclamation of Praise, for all worship is directed first to God and away from ourselves. It has to be reiterated that the primary reason for being at any

* See Appendix (i) for an Order of Service.

service, however important the special occasion may be, is to offer worship to Almighty God.

The Intercessions demonstrate the universality of our concern and the ecumenical spirit in which we meet. Its Christian quality is not demeaned because we pray for people of other faiths and know that they like us are seeking to follow the light that we have been given. The confession of sin and sickness needs fuller explanation and enlargement. First, it requires the right answer to the question: 'Do I sin because I am a sinner or am I a sinner because I have sinned?'

We do not in one sense need forgiveness before we have transgressed. The condition of our sinfulness, however, most certainly needs God's grace before it is exemplified in particular sinful actions. Sins are the symptoms of sinfulness, just as diseases of the body manifest themselves in rashes or spots. To treat the symptoms of physical disease without dealing with their underlying cause is evidently foolish. It ought to be equally evident that dealing with sins without dealing with sinfulness is equally so. Infant Baptism proclaims our need of grace before we have actually erred; it is a recognition of what we call original sin—the most evident of all doctrines, of all human conditions. It does not of course imply guilt. It simply asserts the evident facts of man's fallen state, of his sinful nature and of his need of grace. In the Baptismal rite, this is attested. So at a Healing Service the confession of sin as well as of sickness is all important. The congregation are invited to declare their sinful condition and their sick condition. But there is a wider dimension too. It is not only each individual in his or her own situation, nor even the congregation as a whole. That congregation is representative. It represents all mankind, living and departed. It is apologising to God for all the sinfulness and all the sins that ever were.

The corporate nature of the church, itself a symbol of the fact that all men everywhere belong together, has been all too often forgotten. We have become too self-centred as individuals and as congregations. When Michael Wilson said 'There is no peace for Britain without Bangladesh' he was expressing this vital truth. So our confession of sin and sickness must seek to express the sinful nature and sinful action of the whole family of man, just as it must also tell of our own misdeeds. So at this point we kneel to sing a hymn to the Holy Spirit, in which we pray for insight and self-knowledge. Then collectively and individually our needs are brought to God and we pray for His mercy; we pray for forgiveness and healing; and then we go to the altar for the laying on of hands, for ourselves, for one another, for our neighbours far and near.

Before those who are to minister healing do so, they will themselves be the recipients of the laying on of hands; they too are sinners; they too are sick. They belong just as surely as everyone else to the community which seeks to acknowledge these truths. A failure to recognise this must be an impediment to the work of the Spirit. So priest and people alike kneel to acknowledge their needs, to make their requests known, and to receive whatever God will give them—and always His grace. Some will come especially on behalf of an absent friend or with special intention for the healing of a sick situation; always it is to the fountain of all grace that we come, to God the only healer. The hands of the priest are channels of that grace. As the tap at the sink is the link between the reservoir and the recipient, so the healing mercies of Christ flow through the outstretched hands of those who minister in his name, to the recipient of His grace.

When all have returned to their place, the general absolution is pronounced. To absolve is to release, to set free. God has promised pardon to the penitent and healing to the sick. We lay hold upon His promises, and pray that we may be worthy of them.

The Lord's Prayer is said in thanksgiving and a hymn of praise is sung to the glory of God before the blessing and dismissal are pronounced.

It is generally good that before the Service begins the church should be peaceful and quiet and conversation reduced to a minimum. At the end of the Service the same peaceful atmosphere should be maintained, by the choice of music and the unhurried withdrawal from the building. It is highly desirable that the congregation should meet socially for a while, experiencing the healing community, for that is what the congregation is, and getting to know each other. It must never be forgotten that loneliness and isolation are the cause of much sickness. Meeting together is not an appendage to the occasion but an integral part of it.

CHAPTER XIV

A VISION REALISED

The reader must forgive an element of autobiography in the writing of this final chapter.

> *God moves in a mysterious way*
> *His wonders to perform.*

The Church of England follows the divine precedent! Her system of private patronage is part of the history and sociology of the country. St Marylebone is in the gift of the Crown, and such appointments are made by the Prime Minister's Ecclesiastical Secretary, a civil servant with an office in 10 Downing Street. Thither I went in consequence of a letter asking me if I would like to be considered for the appointment of Rector of St Marylebone. The implications of this invitation were a mystery to me. It was never fully spelt out why I had been invited or what was expected of me. I was left, it seemed to me, to read 'between the lines'.

Some fifteen years before this, while Vicar of St Mark's Coventry, the offer came to me, as Chaplain of the Coventry and Warwickshire Hospital, to read for the newly founded Diploma in Pastoral Studies at Birmingham University. This might be done in a year of full-time study or in two years of part-time. I opted for the latter and devoted three days a week for two academic years to the study of psychology, sociology, pastoral counselling and other subjects all from a theological perspective. There were some hundred days of 'placements' in various agencies—a general hospital, a psychiatric hospital, a probation office, etc.

I learnt a very great deal from this course and my whole

ministry was reorientated as a result of it. The immediate consequence was my appointment as Director of Coventry Samaritans, and for many years I was involved in the work of that
organisation, first in Coventry and later in Bedford, one of the
great pieces of social outreach of the Church in this century.
My move to the Diocese of St Albans resulted in my appointment as Adviser to the Bishop for Hospital Chaplaincies. But
it was not until the suggestion of St Marylebone arose that I
saw where my studies were eventually leading me. St Marylebone is the Parish Church of Harley Street and Hospital
Land. It might well become a centre for the Churches' ministry
of healing. When the offer was finally made I accepted it on
this assumption.

The significance of the crypt of the church for the fulfilment of this ministry came to me in a sort of vision. It is a
huge area, larger than the church itself. It was built as a burial
chamber when the church was built in 1817. By 1850 it was
virtually full, with some 850 bodies laid to rest there. Subsequently they were bricked up in their lead-lined coffins and
left.

Many of those buried there would have been alive when the
church was built and present at its consecration. They would
have taken part in the rejoicing that must have accompanied
that event and seen the church in its initial glory—with a
seating capacity of well over a thousand and Sunday by Sunday
packed with worshippers. What some of them seemed to be
saying to me was 'Restore this church to its former glory. The
living need the space more than the dead.' I had to be obedient
to that vision and the process of conversion began.

The bodies were removed with great respect and reverence
and laid to rest in a lovely part of the forest at Brookwood
Cemetery. A plaque in the church and a memorial cross at
Brookwood both record the fact. Bishop Morris Maddocks and
Dr Martin Israel assisted at a Eucharist of rededication of the
crypt to its new use and of commemoration of those whose
mortal remains had for so long laid there.

But before this could happen funds had to be raised. The removal of the bodies alone cost many thousands of pounds. Professional fund-raisers were consulted and we were indebted to Messrs Craigmyle of Harpenden for setting us off on the right course. I sought the sponsorship of Church, State and Medicine in the persons of the Archbishop of Canterbury, the Lord Chancellor who as a Member of Parliament represented St Marylebone, and Sir Douglas Black, the President of the Royal College of Physicians. All of them readily gave their help. The Duchess of Kent graced a public meeting which was addressed by the Bishop of London to engender interest in what we were seeking to do. Then came the day when the Reverend Richard McLaren was appointed as Appeals Director, and the work of fund-raising was in earnest. We appealed not only for the crypt but also for the restoration of the fabric and for a new organ. Subsequently concern for the fabric was no longer necessary—the work was virtually done—and the new organ was transferred to a separate charitable appeal which would be concerned with the whole of our musical tradition and shared between us and the Royal Academy of Music, situated opposite to the church in the Marylebone Road.

Interest and support were both readily forthcoming. Individual people, charitable trusts, business houses in and beyond the parish, gave most generously and continue to do so. The media showed considerable interest and brought us valuable publicity. The medical profession was intrigued by the concept of a NHS surgery being included in the complex and an article appeared in the *British Medical Journal* as well as references in many other medical periodicals. By now the original idea had been both enlarged and modified and we were to see the final plans drawn up.

The first ingredient in this was of course the extension of the ministry of healing and counselling which was my own commitment. There are many counselling centres in London and many centres of Christian healing. My idea was to extend what had been for so long my own approach, a combination of the insights of spiritual direction and Christian healing with the secular disciplines of case-work and counselling. Prayer, the sacraments (especially unction, the laying on of hands and confession) and pastoral counselling, combined with the insights of psychology and psychiatry—could not these be combined in a holistic approach to those who turn to the Church at their moment of need?

The Church's ministry is not an alternative to medicine but a complement to it. I had long been advocating the appointment of chaplains to General Practices on a comparable basis to their appointment in NHS hospitals. I still think that it is a good idea—despite the obvious difficulties in implementing it. In the crypt however we might appoint a doctor to the chaplain and that was part of the vision. Could it be done? In a 're-stricted area' theoretically adequately doctored, despite the actual difficulty of enrolling on a GP's list, the answer was 'No'. But a way forward was the establishment of a branch surgery by an existing local practice. By providential good fortune, Dr Patrick Pietroni, Chairman of the newly-formed British Holistic Medical Association showed interest and eventually agreed to come. He will bring with him not only a clinical practice but also an educational and a research dimension. He is a lecturer at St Mary's Hospital, Paddington, and attached to a practice at the Lisson Grove Health Centre, which has promised to support him in his move from their premises to the crypt centre.

My interest in complementary medicine is matched by his and we are both members of the Royal Society of Medicine's Colloquium on the relationship between orthodox medicine and some of the leading complementaries. We hope to see osteopathy and acupuncture practised in the crypt complex and we will have a music therapy unit there. The latter affords a bridge between our ministry of healing and the church's long and outstanding musical tradition.

Part of the vision was to invite some of the existing agencies of the Church to come together into the crypt with a view to pooling resources and providing a more comprehensive service. We had some accommodation in the church itself to enable them to begin before the crypt conversion was carried out. The Churches' Council for Health and Healing was first to respond. Brian Frost was then its General Secretary. We made an office available in the old choir vestry and the choir were the first occupants of the crypt in one of the two chambers where there had never been bodies and which could easily be converted to a new use. Soon afterwards the Anglican Guild of St Raphael joined us and shared the newly adapted crypt with the choir, to the inconvenience of neither and with proper economy of space. Then came half of the administration of the Institute of Religion and Medicine, who shared the Sacristy with the clergy, to be joined by the other half a year later, when a new General Secretary was appointed. In the meantime Bishop Morris Maddocks, already Chairman of the Churches' Council for Health and Healing, was appointed Adviser to the Archbishops for Health and Healing, and had his London office at the church.

I have written of an extension of my own ministry into the crypt. At the time of writing I have a small 'case-load' of regular clients whom I see on a weekly or monthly basis. This is backed up by the monthly Healing Service at 6.30 pm on the first Sunday of each month, which draws a large congregation from a wide catchment area. It would be true to say that the church has become a 'pilgrimage centre' for many who come to this Service. But when the crypt is developed there will be regular healing services in the chapel, on a smaller but much more frequent scale. There will also be befrienders and counsellors, trained and prepared to extend the ministry, all day, every day, for people referred to us or on a self-referral basis. I have borrowed the term 'befriender' from the Samaritan organisation as much of my planning owes a great deal to that organisation. The first echelon of help will be befrienders—not qualified but chosen for their innate qualities

of heart and mind, and carefully prepared for the work they
will be doing. Beyond them there will be trained counsellors,
always still on the specific model of overt Christian ministry,
to whom the befriender will refer those who need more
specialised help than they themselves are able to give. Psy-
chotherapy and psychiatry will of course be the ultimate refer-
ence for those who need it. It remains to be seen whether this
will be available on site or only close at hand.

All our work will have the backing of social facilities—a hall
and small restaurant will be provided. The book shop in the
church proper will be available to all who come to the crypt
and to the church. We plan to develop a library. The hall will
be available for lectures, seminars, exhibitions and other
educational activities, whether organised by us, any of the other
'users' or outside bodies who may want to share our facilities.

The vision is five years' old. In January 1987 it will be a
reality, a vision realised.

APPENDIX I

St Marylebone Parish Church

SERVICE OF HEALING

Private Preparation before the Service

*Lord, we remember your presence with us and offer ourselves
to you in Faith and Hope and Love,*

*We believe in your power, both to heal and to save; we pray
that your will may be done, in us and through us.*

*We hope in your promises; we pray that we may be made
worthy of them.*

*We love you and pray that we may love you better, for by
your love we are made and sanctified.*

*We pray for ourselves, for one another and for all mankind,
that we may serve you faithfully and in all things seek
your glory, through Jesus Christ our Lord.   AMEN.*

ORDER OF SERVICE

Jesus said, 'Heal the sick and say, The Kingdom of God
has come near to you'

AN ACCLAMATION OF THANKSGIVING AND PRAISE (*All stand*)

Praise to you, Heavenly Father, Almighty God, Who
created us in your own image and likeness, and holds us
in being by your love.

V. For all your mercies we thank you, Father
R. Blessed be God for ever.

Praise to you, Lord Jesus Christ, Son of the Father,
Who died and rose again, that you might live for ever at
the right hand of the Father, ever to make intercession
for us and for all men.

V. For all your mercies we thank you, Lord
R. Blessed be God for ever.

Praise to you, Holy Spirit of God, Who, proceeding from
the Father, came down upon the Holy Apostles and now
comes into our hearts to make us holy.

V. For all your mercies we thank you, Holy Spirit
R. Blessed be God for ever.

Praise to you Holy and Blessed Trinity, Three Persons
and One God, Who is alive and reigns from eternity to
eternity, and to whom we lift up our hearts in praise and
worship.

V. For all your mercies we thank you, God
R. Blessed be God for ever.

To God the Father, who first loved us, and made us accepted in the Beloved; to God the Son who loves us and washed us from our sins in His own blood; to God the Holy Spirit who sheds the love of God abroad in our own hearts; to Thee, the one true God, be all love and all glory for time and for eternity.   AMEN.

HYMN

INTERCESSION

We pray for all mankind, for the whole family of man, for your children, our brothers and sisters, throughout the world. We pray for all who offer to you the love and worship of their hearts; for Jews and Muslims; for men and women of all faiths believing in you and seeking to serve you, by the light you have granted to them.

V. Lord in your mercy
R. Hear our prayer.

We pray for all Christian people, Catholic, Orthodox, Protestant; for the peace of your Church; for the healing of its schisms; for the unity for which our Lord Jesus Christ Himself prayed.

V. Lord in your mercy
R. Hear our prayer.

We pray for the Church of England and for the other denominations represented here this day; for the mission and ministry of this Church; for the furtherance of our work of healing and counselling.

V. Lord in your mercy
R. Hear our prayer.

We pray for all those who suffer; for the victims of war and violence, of persecution and aggression, of disaster and accident; we pray for the homeless and the hungry;

for the destitute and the oppressed; for the lonely and the unloved; for those who mourn.

V. Lord in your mercy
R. Hear our prayer.

We pray for the sick in our own community, in our hospitals and homes; those who turn to us for healing and comfort; those who are known to us; those who have asked for our prayers.

V. Lord in your mercy
R. Hear our prayer.

We pray for ourselves and for one another that we may mediate healing and be instruments of your peace and joy; we pray for our own healing and salvation.

V. Lord in your mercy
R. Hear our prayer.

COLLECT

O God, who has prepared for those who love you such good things as pass man's understanding: pour into our hearts such love towards you, that we, loving you above all things, may obtain your promises, which exceed all that we can desire, through Jesus Christ our Lord. AMEN.

THE READINGS, followed by **SILENCE**

ANTHEM

ADDRESS

HYMN TO THE HOLY SPIRIT (*Kneeling*)

CONFESSION OF SIN & SICKNESS

Pause for self-examination:

We bring to God our needs. We are, by nature, sinners who need God's grace to live our lives according to His will; we are, by our own fault, sinners who need God's forgiveness for the things we have done which we ought not to have done, and left undone which we ought to have done; we are, by our own fault, by the fault of others, or by the seeming accident of fortune, sick; our sickness may be of the body, of the mind or of the spirit; it may be a sickness in our relationship with ourselves, with other people, with our environment, with God. All these needs we bring before God in penitence and in faith, in sure and certain hope of healing and salvation as He wills for us.

We say together:

God our Father, we bring before you our sins and our diseases; we acknowledge before you our need of your saving Grace. Forgive and heal us according to your gracious promises, that we may serve you in newness of life to the Glory of your Name, through Jesus Christ our Lord.   AMEN.

THE LAYING ON OF HANDS[1] and, where appropriate, THE ANOINTING WITH OIL.[2]

THE ABSOLUTION

Almighty God our Heavenly Father who has promised forgiveness of sins to all who are penitent, and healing to all who are sick; have mercy upon you, pardon and deliver you from all your sins; release you from all sickness and infirmity, and fill you with the grace of His Holy Spirit, through Jesus Christ our Lord. AMEN.

Remember, O Lord, what you have wrought in us, and not what we deserve, and as you have called us to your service, make us worthy of your calling, through Jesus Christ our Lord.   AMEN.

THE LORD'S PRAYER

HYMN

PRAYER & BLESSING

FINAL ANTHEM

1 *At the Laying on of Hands*

May God who made you make you whole
as he would have you be,
in the name and through the power
of the Risen and Ascended Christ,
present with us now in his Holy Spirit.
May he send you forth,
renewed and restored to do his will,
to your benefit, in the service of others,
but above all to the glory of his Holy Name.
AMEN.

2 *At the Anointing*

As outwardly and with sacramental oil
your body is anointed
so may Almighty God, our Father,
inwardly anoint your soul, to strengthen you
with all the comfort and the joy
of his most Holy Spirit,
and to loose you from all that troubles you
in body, mind, or spirit.
May he send you forth,
renewed and restored to do his will,
to your benefit, in the service of others,
but above all to the glory of his Holy Name.
AMEN.

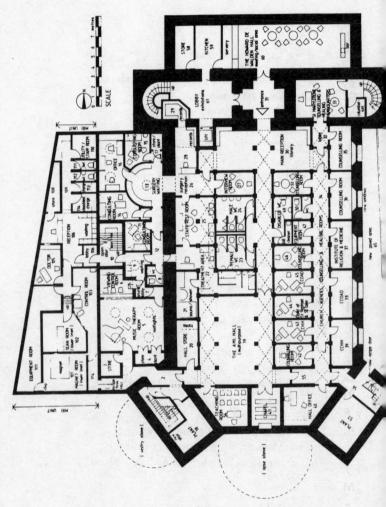

Plan of the St. Marylebone Christian Healing and
Counselling Centre

Also published by ARTHUR JAMES:

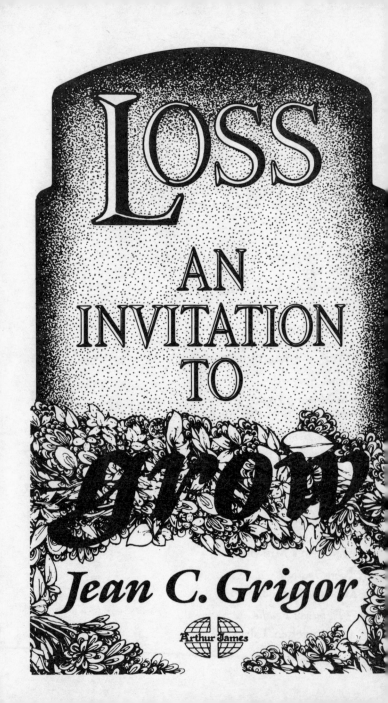